Grant Justice

Lessons Learned Fighting for Justice in the Murder of Oscar Grant

By Keith Muhammad

References

Psalm 94:20 (King James Version)
20Shall the throne of iniquity have fellowship with thee, which frameth mischief by a law?

Isaiah 59:14 (King James Version)
14And judgment is turned away backward, and justice standeth afar off: for truth is fallen in the street, and equity cannot enter.

Holy Qur'an 3:108
These are the messages of Allah which We recite to thee with truth. And Allah desires no injustice to (His) creatures.

Holy Qur'an 4:135
O you who believe, be maintainers of justice, bearers of witness for Allah, even though it be against your own selves or (your) parents or near relatives — whether he be rich or poor, Allah has a better right over them both. So follow not (your) low desires, lest you deviate. And if you distort or turn away from (truth), surely Allah is ever Aware of what you do.

Holy Qur'an 5:80
O you who believe, be upright for Allah, bearers of witness with justice; and let not hatred of a people incite you not to act equitably. Be just; that is nearer to observance of duty. And keep your duty to Allah. Surely Allah is Aware of what you do.

The Muslim Program: What the Muslims Want
6. We want an immediate end to police brutality and mob attacks against the so-called Negro throughout the United States.
We believe that the Federal Government should intercede to see that Black men and women tried in the White courts receive justice in accordance with the laws of the land – or allow us to build a new nation for ourselves, dedicated to justice, freedom and liberty.

Table of Contents

References 2

Acknowledgements 4

I am Oscar Grant 7

Chapter 1: January 1, 2009 9

Chapter 2: The Cover-Up Begins 14

Chapter 3: You-tube and KTVU:
The Shot Heard Around the World 20

Chapter 4: "What are you all doing about this?" 25

Chapter 5: Meet the District Attorney 29

Chapter 6: Rebellion and the Mayor 36

Chapter 7: Activism, Townhall Meetings,
and the Caravan for Justice 41

Chapter 8: Oakland on Trial 52

Chapter 9: Preliminary Hearing, Change of Venue,
Rodney King and Oscar Grant 57

Chapter 10: Trial 64

Chapter 11: The Verdict 72

Chapter 12: Justice 84

Timeline 93

Acknowledgements

In the name of ALLAH, the Beneficent, the Merciful. I bear witness there is no God but ALLAH and I bear witness that Muhammad is His Messenger.

I am a student of the Teachings of the Most Honorable Elijah Muhammad, and I could never thank ALLAH enough for His Intervention in our affairs in the Person of Master Fard Muhammad, and for His raising the Honorable Elijah Muhammad to lead, teach, and guide us out of darkness into the true and marvelous light of God. I thank ALLAH for their National Representative, a Divine man of God to whom I owe my life and purpose to, my leader and Guide, whom I represent to the city of Oakland, the Honorable Minister Louis Farrakhan. Thank you for your Love, Guidance and the opportunity to serve.

To my wife, Salamah: Surely, no man can engage a world of struggle without one to give him comfort and peace of mind. There are not enough pages in this writing to say thanks to ALLAH for you. You stand steadfastly by my side through sickness and in health, for richer or for poorer, for long as we both shall live. No man has ever had a loving woman like you. Thank you, dear.

To my mother: You feared when I accepted Islam that my face would be in the news, that I would rise into a leadership position, and that I would be marked or black listed. I did my best to comfort your motherly concerns, but I must walk the path that God set me upon. I thank God for your husband, Willie Bolden. His profound love and care for you remain deeply rooted in my heart.

To my oldest son, Salih, who is becoming a great helper in the cause of truth. To Ismail, whose faithful and loving spirit keeps a smile on my face. To Jabril, whose caution, yet fearless fighting spirit always encourages me to know that our Nation has a bright future. To Zahir, who has grown up in Townhall meetings and expects to see his father striving for justice. May ALLAH bless you to increase in your service to the people of God. I love you.

To the Believers at Muhammad Mosque #26B: You have been the wind beneath my wings. Your sacrifice has allowed me to travel in the journey for justice. Thank you to the Laborers of Islam in Oakland, who are engaged in the very real struggle of helping the Minister in the Resurrection of our people. I thank you for your prayers, your sacrifices, and your life in service to the people of God. Thank you to Brother Kimara, Brother Gary, Sister Michelle and Sister Beatrice for your help. Special thanks to the Believers who have taken the lead in the journey for justice by attending mosque meetings, Townhall meetings, public hearings, the Caravans for Justice, and donated time, talent, skills, money and love to help in the Journey for Justice.

Special thanks also to the many Believers in the Nation of Islam who have offered encouragement to me as we fight the good fight. I knew at any time there were men of integrity, sons of thunder, willing and able to pick up the stick and carry us to the finish line. Thank you to my brothers in the Ministry Class of the Honorable Minister Louis Farrakhan. To Brother Christopher Muhammad and Brother Tony Muhammad, Allah willing, we are all links in a chain in the West so strong that even the devil wished that he could be a part of this. Thanks for the support, guidance and love. Whenever I feel down, I can count on ALLAH to send you to lift me up with your loving support and beautiful spirits.

I thank Allah for the helpers who participated in preparing this book. Many thanks belong to Sisters Erika Muhammad and Vivian X for your editing help. Thanks to Brothers Gene Hazzard, Reginald James, Jamo Muhammad, and Victor Muhammad for your photography; and to Dr. Siri Brown, Sisters Valita Jones, Tonja Muhammad and Anne Williams for your support in preparing this book. Thank you to Brother Dawood Muhammad for the cover art.

To Jack Bryson, whose sons watched as Johannes Mehserle murdered their brother: I love your spirit, your compassion, and your pursuit of justice.

This journey produced a team of activist thinkers who committed themselves to unite in the cause of justice. I thank ALLAH for all those who sacrifices brought us this far in pursuit of justice. Thank you.

To Wanda and Cephus Johnson, Chantay Moore, Tatiana and Sophina Mesa: it has been my honor and duty to serve your family in the Journey for Justice. This is a path I accepted long before we ever met, and in truth, we all were placed on this path long before any of us were born into the world. We live in a journey prepared for us by God; therefore, no matter how difficult the road may seem, we have the strength to bear. It is with love of God and love for life that I serve you and the community.

I am Oscar Grant
(Reflections from the Johnson Family)

Kenny Johnson, uncle of Oscar Grant

Oscar came to stay with me one summer, and the thing that I liked the most was how respectful he was to me my wife and my house. There was not one thing that I told him to do that he did not do. He always had a smile on his face and didn't complain. We spent most evenings talking and laughing, playing cards and dominos, and just enjoying his company in the house. There was never a time when I came to visit my family that he didn't make time to come see me and my wife. One thing I will say about Oscar is he valued family. That was an important part of his life. He was the type of young man that was loved by many and was known by many as the kind of man that once you met him; you met a good guy that you would enjoy being around.

Cephus Johnson, affectionately known as Uncle Bobby

"My letter to you, my nephew Oscar"

You were a beautiful, happy baby nephew. The moment I saw your smile it brought much joy to my spirit. It was like you knew you had work to do and it would be your smile that you would do it with. Your smile would light up a room. Your smile would bring joy to a bad day. It was a toothy smile. That smile that you came into this world with was the same spirited smile that you left me with. It was as though you knew, before you caught that BART Train, it would be your last day of life to smile for your uncle. It was as though you were saying, "uncle I Love you, and I must go now". It was that same spirited smile, that transported itself to my spirit, where I was prompted in my spirit to text you at 12:49 am, one hour and ten minutes before you were murdered, texting " Uncle Loves You, God Loves you, God Loves your family".

Your beautiful spirited smile has touched everyone you have come in contact with. It's that same spirited smile that we see in all the music, art, poetry, and spoken word that was inspired by your sacrifice. Your smile will live in me for the rest of my life. You have shared with the world your spirit and your smile. People have said thank you to your family for your gift of Life, your beautiful spirit, and your beautiful smile.

It will be because of your Love for Life, by your beautiful smile that will bring your tragic death to an ending with a victory for Justice. Uncle misses you. Uncle loves you. Uncle says thank you. I will always remind the world that you were murdered and the criminal justice system will have to hold Johannes Mehserle accountable for the murder he committed. It is God's word that I will stand on,

"Hebrews 11:6 But without faith [it is] impossible to please [him:] for he that cometh to God must believe that he is, and [that] he is a rewarder of them that diligently seek him ".

May the Peace of God guide all of us, in all that we do, with the remembrance of your spirited smiling face. I love you.

Uncle Bobby

Chapter 1
January 1, 2009

Courtesy of Johnson Family

On January 1, 2009, Oscar Grant III, his fiancé' and friends travelled on Bay Area Rapid Transit (BART), seeking to enjoy the New Years' Celebrations in San Francisco, California. Before leaving the birthday celebration of his mother, Wanda Johnson, Oscar was asked by his mother not to drive to San Francisco, but to catch BART. Like many concerned mothers, Wanda felt that riding BART would be the safest way to travel on a holiday night, where drinking and driving bring special law enforcement out to detain and arrests many drivers.

Oscar obeyed his mother's loving guidance. He and his companions traveled to and from San Francisco aboard a packed train. A passenger got into a minor pushing match with Oscar. The dispute was settled on the train and Oscar and his friends got off the train at the Fruitvale Station in Oakland, where they were approached by an angry, yelling, taser wielding police officer, Tony Pirone.

Officer Pirone directed the group to move against a wall and wait for him. Most of the young men that were still present, complied. Oscars' fiancé; the mother of his child, Sophina Mesa, had already gone downstairs after departing the train. She would never again see Oscar Grant III, her loving fiancé'and the father of their 4 year old daughter, Tatiana.

Oscar and his friend, Michael Greer, watched the aggression in the manner of Officer Tony Pirone and attempted to avoid him. They re-boarded the BART train. Officer Pirone shouted orders for the young men to get off the train. Pirone did not know who he was searching for beyond the brief call that said Black men had been in a fight aboard the train. Pirone escalated his aggression and declared, "Get off of my fucking train." Oscar complied. Pirone walked him to the wall where his other friends had been detained.

Officer Marisol Domenici, Pirone's partner was left to watch Oscar Grant and his young friends along the BART station wall. Together at the wall with Oscar are Jackie Bryson (22), Nigel Bryson (18), and Carlos Reyes (21).

Pirone boarded the train, shouted at Greer to get off the fucking train. Eventually, Greer surrendered himself to Pirone. An angry and abusive Pirone, snatched Greer by the hair and wrist. He pulls him to the wall nearest to Oscar and his friends, and proceeded to throw a non-resistant Greer at the retaining wall.

When Greer bounced off the wall, Pirone then snatched Greer by his dreadlocks, placed his knee behind Greer's' and slammed him to the ground, in a maneuver Pirone would later boast his skills for in court, and called it a classic hair-take down move.

Having witnessed their friend, subjected to unnecessary force and abuse, Oscar and his friends began to question the officers and complained that they had not done anything wrong. They wanted to know why Pirone was beating on their friend Michael. Out of concern for the safety of their friend Michael, they spoke out.

Officer Domenici told the young men to leave it alone, not to interfere, and be quiet. As Oscar continued to complain and he stood on his feet to further inquire and talk to Officer Domenici. As they spoke, Pirone left Greer and shouted at Oscar to "sit the fuck down" and knocked Oscar down with an aggressive forearm shiver.

Oscar was struck by Pirone for the first time. Oscar submitted to further instruction and sat down. After he sat and complained about being mistreated, BART police back-up arrived on the crime scene. Officer Johannes Mehserle joined other BART officers in supporting the actions of Officer Tony Pirone.

Pirone returned to Greer to place handcuffs on him. As Oscar and friends complained and questioned the officers over this abusive behavior. Mehserle pulled his taser and points it at Oscar Grant. Oscar gets on his cell phone and called his fiancé. He told her the police were beating them up for nothing, pointed his cell phone camera and took his final picture. He took a picture of Johannes Mehserle pointing a taser weapon right at him.

After cuffing Greer, Pirone told Mehserle to handcuff Oscar. Oscar had done nothing unlawful. He only had the courage to verbally question the officers. His only crime was being unafraid to speak.

Pirone decided he would make an example of Oscar. This young man had the nerve to question his actions in front of his partner, Marisol Domenici.

He told Mehserle to cuff Oscar and as Oscar sat on his knees against the BART station wall, Pirone shouted the racially offensive epithets, "Bitch ass nigger right. Bitch ass nigger right."

Officer Mehserle grabbed Oscar by the shoulders and threw Oscar down onto his face and stomach. Pirone was so pleased to see Oscar in a position at his feet that he shouted with pleasure, "Yeah"

Oscar fell across the feet of his friend, Carlos Reyes. His hands were trapped beneath his body, which was lying across the feet of Carlos. As Mehserle and Pirone struggled to pull Oscar's arms from beneath him, Carlos yelled, "He's on my leg. He's on my leg."

Evidently, Pirone realized the awkward position and picked Oscar up from Carlos' foot and laid him flat on the pavement. Then, Pirone put his knees in the back of Oscar's neck, shoulders and head. Pirone was a body builder and former Marine, who weighed more than 235 pounds. Mehserle took a position near Oscar's waist and like Pirone, placed the force of his 6'5, 260 pound frame across the back of a 5 foot 10 inch, 170 pound Oscar Grant.

Within 30 seconds, Mehserle inexplicably released Oscars' hands, stood up, carefully drew and aimed his weapon, and fired the fatal bullet into the lower back, killing Oscar Grant.

Oscar was so shocked that he'd been shot, that he spoke his final words to his killer, Johannes Mehserle, saying, "You shot me? You shot me?

How to Respond When Stopped by Police

Read *What to Do When Stopped By Police* by the National Association of Black Law Enforcement Officers, Inc. http://www.nableo.org/publications/whattodo_whenstopped.pdf

1. What are your rights when stopped by police?
2. How should you exercise those rights when confronted by an apparently rogue police officer?

Hayward Police on full alert for a rally for Oscar Grant in February 2009; celebrating Oscar's birthday. Oscar was born on Febraury 27. Photo: Gene Hazzard

Chapter 2
The Cover-Up Begins

Photo: Gene Hazzard

The first actions taken by BART cops after the murder of Oscar Grant were the actions that verified their intention to cover the tracks of Johannes Mehserle.

Much ado has been made of the argument that Mehserle was shocked by the shooting of Oscar. His attorney argued that we know Mehserle was shocked because of his words and facial expression. After shooting Oscar he put his hands near his face, looked dumbfounded and said, "O Shit!"

However, though claiming to be shocked, Mehserle calmly leaned over to Oscar, put his knee into Oscar's back, near his wounds, and proceeded to handcuff the man he claims to have shot by accident.

There was not a police policy that said, handcuff the man you've accidentally killed or wounded. An accidental shooting demands a humane response. Mehserle did not offer a response that respected Oscar's humanity. He issued a cold, letter of the law, measured policy response. He cuffed a man he later claimed to have both accidentally shot, yet feared was reaching for a gun. Many times I have heard Uncle Bobby, Oscar's uncles Cephus Johnson, describe that as Oscar was lifted from the ground in handcuffs, that his friends saw blood and gun smoke flow from the body of their friend.

Many of us were aware of a citizens' right against self-incrimination. Like all citizens in America, Mehserle was lawfully protected from self-incrimination. The so-called Peace Officers Bill of Rights offers to law enforcement officers in California protection from interview in the absence of an attorney. In Mehserle's case, not only did he await an attorney, his attorney did not allow him to offer an explanation to his employer for an on duty shooting. He simply signed a modified form acknowledging that he'd fired his weapon that night. No statement of who was shot and why ever occurred between BART and Mehserle.

The officers at the scene of the crime were eventually interviewed, but their reports were incomplete and vague. No BART officer testified to seeing or hearing a gun shot. BART cops, including Mehserle would later testify to hearing "loud sounds", "strange sounds", "loud noises", and even claimed to hear a taser malfunction. The cover-up was clearly being prepared and shared in reports for later testimony; not even Johannes Mehserle claimed to hear his own gun fire.

BART conducted its internal affairs investigation of a shooting without the report of the officer responsible for the shooting. The chief of BART police, Gary Gee made no effort to compel Mehserle to report his actions. I asked Chief Gee what power or authority he had with reference to disciplining an officer who failed to report his conduct while working. He told me that he could have charged Mehserle with insubordination. Then, I asked him if he charged Mehserle with insubordination, Gee dropped his head and voice and answered, "No." As a result, BART took no action against Mehserle for shooting Oscar Grant. No reprimand, no warning, no dissatisfaction; nothing. BART did nothing to demonstrate its feeling that Mehserle was wrong. The chief of police supported Mehserle and avoided the pursuit of justice.

How is it possible, in the midst of such tragedy, that the head is not in contact with the body? Chief Gee was more interested in keeping the espirit de corps of his officers than pursuing truth. As a result, while his former officer, who resigned to avoid interview, sat in Santa Rita Jail, Gee sent a letter to BART police officers with its police union representative, urging officers to send money, letters of support, and whatever encouragement they could for Johannes Mehserle in Santa Rita jail.

In fact, as we sat and questioned Mr. Gee, the letter of support reached my email and caused my phone to buzz. The meeting was so important that I did not look at the phone, but Pastor Harold Mayberry of First AME Church was aware and brought this to our attention. Again, Chief Gee dropped his head and admitted that was his signature on the letter and perhaps it was not the wisest thing to do.

The beginning of the cover for Mehserle was underway. Mehserle told Officer Pirone that he thought Oscar may have been reaching for a gun. To protect his legal right, Mehserle was assigned an officer by BART to act as a counselor, friend and aid. This officer drove Mehserle from Oakland to Sacramento and back to meet his attorney. On the ride, Mehserle repeated that he thought Oscar had a gun. According to the testimony of his fellow officer, not one time did Mehserle say to his friend and BART official companion, "I thought I was pulling my taser" in the hours they spent riding to Sacramento to see his lawyers.

When Mehserle was finally arrested two weeks after the shooting and arrived in court for arraignment, his attorney stated that Mehserle thought Oscar had a gun.

16

The taser defense was never made until video evidence emerged and was broadcast over internet and reached television news outlets. Like Rodney King, this case would reach the public attention by way of published video from BART passengers. The first video, made available by a real hero, Karina Vargas, set forth an avalanche of activity. These images painted far more than a thousand words. The eventual revelation of multiple videos and photos made by Katarina Vargas, Tommy Cross, Jamil Dewar, BART platform cameras and even the last cell phone picture taken by Oscar Grant, this case would be seen by the world. The taser defense appeared to be the invention of Mehserle's lawyers.

Many other cases of police brutality go without public outcry. Police internal affairs department are just that; internal. The shame is that internal affairs would be appropriate if a police officer failed to obey an order from commanding officers, arrived late for work repeatedly, accumulated enough parking tickets to have his car towed and talked to his friends in the traffic division to give him a break. These would require internal affairs because they are internal. But once the offense committed involves the public this is no longer an internal affair; rather, it becomes a matter of public safety and equal protection rights under the law. Public safety should not be relegated to "internal affairs", it is now an "external" affair with negative impacts on the innocent. Privacy rights of employees (police) should not override my human and civil right to life and equal protection. Does a citizen have an equal right to protection from unlawful actions of a police officer?

The Oakland Police Department, though not involved in the shooting of Oscar Grant provides us a glimpse into the problems of police-community relationships. It is currently under monitor of a Federal Court for the wayward actions of its police Department. A group of rogue elements inside the Department known as the Riders were brought to court and criminally charged for abuses of the public for false arrests, false reports, kidnapping, and planting evidence. After the four officers were charged, the apparent ring leader fled the country and has yet to return to face trial. The other 3 were tried and acquitted, being defended by Mehserle's attorney, Michael Rains. The City of Oakland has been left with millions of dollars in settlements as a result of police brutality settlements.

Federal Court Judge Thelton Henderson, responsible for oversight since the Negotiated Settlement Agreement of 2003 has declared his disappointment with OPD for its failure to comply with reform orders mandated by the court. The primary for reform was the

Internal Affairs department. Police departments do not police themselves well. The Oakland Police Department received hundreds of citizen complaints and seemingly ignored them. This kind of police inaction when necessary to correct and discipline its own has led to community demands for civilian review. BART police had no system worth mentioning for its riders to make a complaint against its officers.

Hayward Police response to the family of Oscar Grant at this February 2009 rally. Photos:Gene Hazzard

1. What is the role of the department of internal affairs?

2. What is civilian review?

3. What cities have civilian review boards for their police department? What are their powers?

Christopher Muhammad addresses the BART Board of Directors
Photo: Victor Muhammad

Chapter 3
You-tube and KTVU:
The Shot Heard Around the
World

In the early morning hours of March 3, 1991, a Los Angeles motorist, Rodney King, was severely beaten by members of the Los Angeles Police Department. The name Rodney King has become synonymous with the term, police brutality. Rodney King was not the first, nor was he the last, to suffer from an attack by a mob of police. What made his case significantly different from any other beating was the presence of a video camera. George Holliday, a resident near the beating was home learning how to use his new camera and noticed the action below his apartment. Police brutality by members of America's best known police force was broadcast for the world to see.

Los Angeles is still recovering from the reaction to the case that resulted in the trial of King's abusers being moved out of Los Angeles County, public dispute between the cities mayor and police chief, and the eventual revolt that left large parts of the city burning. No one wanted to see this kind of incident ever again.

On the morning of January 3rd, news of Oscar Grant's shooting death was beginning to buzz through word of mouth in the community. Local newspapers were stating that Grant had been killed aboard BART, but there was no real description of what happened. Black men, many of whom have been confronted by racial profiling and have suffered rush to judgment where police violence is concerned were naturally suspicious.

Unfortunately, the complaints of young Black men who are victims of police brutality are often met with skepticism. Many immediately assumed that Grant must have done something wrong. Was he a drunken New Years' reveler? Was he a dangerous gang member? Was he a fighting dope dealer? Stereotypes flooded the mind.

Fortunately, on the morning of January 3rd, a group of conscientious men gathered at Olivet Missionary Institutional Baptist Church. These brothers met to discuss the issues that lead to our community destruction: mass incarceration, gentrification, poor training and miseducation of Black youth, and environmental racism. We were in the midst of looking at these issues and seeking to organize ourselves to address them effectively as a community.

Minister Christopher Muhammad, a driving force in the Bay Area in organizing action, was the keynote speaker. As we met and discussed the issues, I began to ask the brothers if they had any information about the shooting. Unfortunately, no one was well informed. The news was just reaching the press, but again, no video.

On my way home from the meeting, I received a call from Saleem Muhammad, asking had I seen the news of the shooting; that a young, unarmed brother was shot and it was on tape.

That night, the video began picking up attention in all the news networks. You-tube played and replayed the murder. Buzz was building all over the area about the shooting.

Like many other Sunday's, I prepared for our weekly mosque meeting. After our spiritual meeting, I went home and prepared for my Monday activity. We were planning a Townhall meeting in East Oakland at Arroyo Viejo Park where Councilperson Desley Brooks welcomed us into its community center. At this point, the video of Oscar's killing was heating up the community. No one had spoken publically from among Black leadership.

Attendance at the meeting was low, so we had a smaller planning meeting with Ms. Brooks, strategizing how to improve condition for the suffering poor in East Oakland.

We talked briefly about the shooting. We acknowledged that we were ignorant to the details and agreed that we would look into the issue and share whatever we found.

The unstated heroes in the journey for justice are the many persons who filmed the murder of Oscar Grant. Several of their records made it into evidence. Even though BART had its own cameras, their recording would most likely have been used as police department cameras are used, and that it's to validate and confirm their right actions during an arrest.

The Rodney King tape was not revealed by LAPD; it was revealed by local media who received it directly from the witness. This case was made by the Vargas video, the Cross video, Oscar's own camera, and the multiple passengers who boldly lifted their phones to record. Were it not for their record, we would never have seen a murder to protest. This case, like most police shootings, would have left many to wonder, "Who do you trust with testimony: young Black men with some stains on their records, or police officers, sworn to protect the public?"

Sworn officers rarely have their word rejected, and young brothers' word is rarely accepted.

Television broadcasts and YouTube have now brought the reality of police brutality before the eyes of the world. What could possibly explain this senseless shooting? What excuse did BART police give for the shooting of an unarmed man, face down beneath the weight of two large cops? What justification will we hear this time?

Any person who ever doubted the explanation of a victim of abuse, beaten, arrested or killed at the hands of law enforcement, on this day, had no excuse to reject standing for justice. One would have to lie to themselves to watch this video and leave the viewing with any suspicion that Oscar was wrong and earned this shooting for his wrong.

According to video evidence and the testimony of many others, Oscar did everything asked of him from the moment he made contact with police. He stood against the wall. Oscar sat and kneeled. Oscar laid face down on the BART station floor as commanded. As a final act of compliance, Oscar put his hands behind his back to be hand cuffed and in the moment he was shot.

YouTube and KTVU broadcast a murder. The execution of an innocent man was made available for the entire world to witness. Millions of internet users have viewed the killing of Oscar Grant. Unlike any other killing in history, this horrific murder was made known to the public almost immediately. None of us could claim these things are relics of the past; we were invited into the pain of police brutality in the present. Televised evidence marked the beginning of a revolution.

1. Since the time of this murder, some states have entertained making it unlawful for citizens to record police actions. Why do you think some are pursuing this kind of law?
2. What action did the Black Panther Party take in response to police brutality in Oakland?
3. What is Copwatch?
4. How do you think the public may have responded to the killing of Oscar Grant if there were no video broadcast?
5. How do you think government may have responded to this killing if there were no video broadcast?

The Caravan for Justice hears from Copwatch.
Photo: Jamo Muhammad

Chapter 4:
"What are you all doing about this?"

Photo: Gene Hazzard

The following Monday night, January 5, Brother Christopher called me, after having seen the video. He inquired what I knew about the killing. Had I seen the tape? My answer was, yes.

The most important question he asked, however, was, "Aren't you part of a group of Black elected officials and pastors? What are you all doing about this? He said that he saw a Latino girl on the news passing out fliers demanding justice and attorney John Burris gave his commentary, but what are the leaders doing to address this murder?

Brother Christopher suggested that I call the leaders together for an emergency meeting to learn what has happened and plan a response. Certainly, we could not consider ourselves community leadership without giving voice to this tragedy. I agreed and called Alameda County Supervisor Keith Carson, Oakland Councilperson Brooks and others.

We met for the first time on Tuesday, January 6, 2009 at Olivet with a circle of about 20 community activists, Councilperson Brooks, staffs from elected officials, and concerned people. While meeting, we were all clearly outraged by another senseless shooting of an unarmed brother, but ignorant to details. We knew that charges should be pursued and arrests should be made, so Councilperson Brooks, an attorney herself, called the District Attorney Tom Orloff.

Ms. Brooks got the district attorney on the phone, stepped out for privacy, and began to inquire about what happened. She told us that she had him on the phone and asked us what we wanted to do. We told her we wanted to meet him, ASAP, to learn the role his office would take in this apparent crime.

Mr. Orloff resisted. He did not want to meet with anyone. After overcoming his resistance, Ms. Brooks let us know he was willing to meet, but that he would only meet 3 from the group. She conveyed to us that he agreed to meet only 3 persons, knowing that we would not accept the offer.

District Attorney Orloff underestimated the power of this group. While we did not have an organization with a name; we did not have a president, chairman and board of directors, this group had a heart that yearned for justice. Ms. Brooks knew our answer before she asked the question. If we accepted this weak response she would have been disappointed in the lack of courage in the room full of men. We **all** wanted to meet and question District Attorney Orloff. Splitting the group into parts was not an option.

We immediately set the stage for a press conference on the steps of the Alameda County Courthouse for the morning of Wednesday, January 7th. Then, after expressing our outrage and demands, we intended to take our meeting, all of us, to the office of the District Attorney.

This small group of activists, pastors, and elected officials were intent on making our demands for justice clear. We all knew that what happened to Oscar Grant could have happened to any one of us or our children. It was clear that were it not for the Grace of God, any of us could have lost our lives that fateful day. Minister Christopher declared, "I am Oscar Grant." This would become the rallying cry for our press conference and eventually for the movement.

We spread the word to our organizations of people for support. It would not be good to present such strong demands without strong support. Believers from mosques in Northern California responded to the call made by Brother Christopher. Church leaders and elected officials responded to my call. The media, on the morning of the funeral of Oscar Grant were contacted with the help of the wife of Rev. Dr. Lawrence Van Hook, Sister Patricia Van Hook, coordinated by Rev. Dion Evans at the press conference and the drive on the Journey for Justice began.

Immediately after our challenge to the District Attorney, concerned activists began planning for justice. Pastors, elected officials, civil rights veterans and others began weekly discussions. Weekly meetings in the home of Ann Williams, coffee shops, businesses, churches and mosques became central places for organizing. I have never experienced such diversity in planning. Few could imagine coming into a coffee shop managed by Black Muslim followers of Minister Farrakhan hosting white, brown, red and yellow activists working harmoniously in pursuit of justice. These planners and thinkers produced an untelevised revolution.

1. Do citizens have a right to question government officials like the District Attorney Orloff, Councilperson Brooks or Supervisor Keith Carson? Are elected officials off limits from our concerns?
2. By what means can you communicate your concerns to government?
3. What institution or organizations exists in your community to respond to tragedies such as this? If none, are you willing to start such a group?

January 7, 2009 Press Conference at the Alameda County Court. Brother Antwayne Muhammad, Pastor Lawrence Van Hook, Brother Keith Muhammad, Rev. Daniel Buford, Rev. Dr. J. Alfred Smith, Sr., Councilperson Desley Brooks
Photo: Gene Hazzard

Chapter 5
Meet the District Attorney

The word went out of our intentions to meet the press. The Black elected officials and faith based leaders sent out word. Youth activists sent out word. Clergy leaders sent out word. The Nation of Islam sent out word.

That morning, over 100 leaders and their supporters arrived on the steps of the Alameda County Courthouse for a 9:00 a.m. press conference. Included were legendary clergy leader, Reverend Dr. J. Alfred Smith, Sr., City Councilperson Desley Brooks, Reverend Dr. Lawrence Van Hook, Pastor Dion Evans, Reverend Zachery Carey, Reverend Brondon Reems, Reverend Daniel Buford, Reverend Dr. Harold Mayberry, Bishop Keith Clark, representatives from the offices of Congressperson Barbara Lee, Assemblyman Sandre Swanson, Supervisor Keith Carson, Mayor Ronald Dellums, state representatives from the NAACP, and members and ministers from the Nation of Islam throughout the Bay Area.

This impressive group made our demands that charges be brought, and a full and transparent investigation and justice secured. Councilperson Desley Brooks addressed the crowd and media and suggested that this was an execution and it should be stated as such. She made a passionate appeal and demanded that the District Attorney respect his constituency and prosecute all involved in the murder of Oscar Grant to the fullest extent of the law. She suggested that this should be the last time Mr. Orloff run for office unopposed. She concluded by reminding us that Oscar Grant was a father who begged for his life. She asked, "Who was there to protect Oscar Grant?"

It was at this press conference that Reverend Lawrence Van Hook repeated the mantra, "I am Oscar Grant." The phrase got all of our attention, and from that moment, speaker after speaker repeated the now infamous phrase, "I am Oscar Grant."

The Reverend Dr. J. Alfred Smith, Sr. appealed to the hearts of the people by making it plain what the community lost. A daughter lost her father. A mother lost her son. A community lost its trust in law enforcement to provide its citizens with protection. He posed the questions, "What should we tell his daughter? What should we tell our sons? Should we tell them to fear the law? Is the law their enemy? If Oscar Grant is not safe, then I am not safe!"

Today, incidents of police brutality all over the country, finds people representing this phrase. Oscar Grant's name is sounded in police conflicts all over the country. Lovelle Mixon/Oscar Grant. Mumia Abu Jamal/Oscar Grant. Parnell Smith/Oscar Grant. Brownie Polk/Oscar Grant. Sean Bell/Oscar Grant. Amadou Diallo/Oscar Grant. Oscar's name is now attached to the journey for justice forever.

This rally was unusually diverse and united. Muslims, Christians, politicians, revolutionaries, youth, elders.

After the press conference and rally, members of the delegation then divided; part traveling to Hayward to honor Oscar and his family at the funeral, others, going to the District Attorney to honor Oscar by demanding Justice.

District Attorney Orloff was confronted by 100 activists in the lobby outside his office. We made our request to the office secretary, and she alerted him to the presence of the crowd. District Attorney Orloff evidently recognized the magnitude of the issue. Surely, the press was calling him for information and simultaneously reporting our demands.

The crowd of activists grew increasingly impatient, yet respectfully voiced our opinions. Chants of No Justice, No Peace rang through the halls of justice. Minister Christopher declared, "This community has been disrespected for too long and at a certain point, enough is enough!"

Mr. Orloff's initial response was to call County Supervisor Keith Carson for help. He did not want to meet with us. He did not know most of us. He probably did not like many of us, so he called for help.

Supervisor Carson, president of the organization of Black elected officials in the East Bay, was surely aware that we were there and what we wanted. He wanted what we wanted: Justice for the Murder of Oscar Grant. However, Supervisor Carson shared with me that because of the county budget crisis, as chairman of the budget meeting, there was no way he could break away and join us that morning. But the District Attorney called him in distress.

Before Brother Carson went in to ease the District Attorney's fears, he asked me what I wanted him to do. I shared with him that our demand was only to meet with District Attorney Orloff to ask him what his office was doing about the videotaped murder of Oscar Grant. Supervisor Carson took Reverend Dr. Smith into a meeting with the District Attorney.

They emerged from the meeting saying the District Attorney would now be willing to meet eight of us, the number he said he could accommodate in his office. We demanded he meet us all. Eight was not acceptable to the group. It was all or nothing at all, although clearly, we had no intentions of not having this critical meeting for justice.

We agreed that I should go into the meeting with Supervisor Carson and Reverend Smith to convey the feeling of the group. Neither Carson nor Smith were in the initial planning meeting and may have knowingly or unwittingly compromised on an issue the group was not willing to compromise. In fact, some of the crowd, seeing them enter the District Attorney's office, began calling them "sell-outs," "Negroes," and "uncle tom's" while watching them enter the doors of the office. It was certainly a very tense time.

As we discussed the importance of meeting the crowd, it appeared that my presence with the District Attorney appeared less threatening to him when he recognized that both Carson and Smith respected me and submitted to our leadership on this issue. So we began to search for a meeting place. The District Attorney was adamant that he was not going out into that crowd or mob. I inquired about the use of an empty court room, conference room, or Laney College. Eventually, the District Attorney agreed to use his conference room.

We emerged from the meeting to say to the crowd, we are ready to meet. We squeezed the remaining crowd into the District Attorney's conference room. Squeezed in between a large conference table and legal books and records were men, women, and children who wanted answers from this District Attorney. As we met, the Chief of Staff to the Mayor quietly joined us; the mayor's personal security came in and sat. Congressperson Lee and Assemblyman Swanson also had staff in the room.

This meeting, like the shooting of Oscar, was taped. Hip-hop legendary reporter Davey D Cook kept his camera rolling. Muslim sisters kept their cell phone cameras ready.

It was in this meeting that District Attorney Orloff acknowledged that his office was investigating the case and believed that in time, charges would be brought against Mehserle. We jammed him about why Mehserle was allowed to walk away without first being questioned. It was then that he told us of the unique relationship between law enforcement and the District Attorney's office. He shared that police are given time to work out their defense.

It was clear to us that this time was given to police to build up their false defense and their lies. We asked the District Attorney whether he would have allowed us time to build up our legal defense if we had killed someone on video, or would he issue an arrest warrant and make us figure out our defense while behind bars.

The District Attorney knew he was wrong and up against a tough crowd. He let us know that he wanted to first build up a strong case and this was why he claimed to take his time about making an arrest. He proceeded to tell us this would take him about two weeks.

Though we disagreed, we acknowledge we were at a stalemate, but then challenged him to tell the public that his office intends to investigate and bring charges against Mehserle. The District Attorney's response offended us all. He said, "I'm not telling anybody anything; you do it."

Supervisor Brooks chided him for not being willing, as a public servant, to share his intentions with his constituents. We all felt that if he did not declare his intention, then his intention was really to do nothing. Another cop would walk away and the news would be declared another justifiable homicide. His position would only encourage people to take justice into their own hands. Later that day, this is exactly what happened: street justice. This was the unhinged anger of a people justifiably angry. We left the meeting angry and searching for the next step.

Later, other activists hosted a rally at the Fruitvale BART Station. Hundreds of people gathered, including men, women, children, and supporters who missed the funeral of Oscar to demand justice. After hours of taking over that station, where activists invited our group to speak, the rally ended peacefully and without conflict.

Some activists at the rally, however, wanted more. They decided to march from the BART station toward downtown Oakland. Police blocked streets, confronted protesters, and then the riots began.

1. What is the Police Bill of Rights?

2. Why did the founding fathers add the Bill of Rights to the U.S. Constitution?

District Attorney Tom Orloff responds to community, January 7, 2009.
Photo: Victor Muhammad

Chapter 6
Rebellion and the Mayor

Photo: Thomas Hawke

After a long day with the press conference, meeting with the DA and rally at Fruitvale, I prepared to teach Islam at the mosque meeting that evening. As I got into my lecture, at about 8:30 p.m., Minister Christopher Muhammad called my cell. Since I was lecturing, I ignored the phone. I didn't even look to see who called. After repeated efforts to reach me, Brother Christopher called my Captain, Gary Muhammad, who approached me on stage with a cell phone in his hand.

My mind raced. I couldn't imagine why he would come to me on stage with a cell phone. The only time I had ever seen this happen was when Minister Farrakhan sent correction to speakers in our national webcasts. I knew it had to be something big, because I would never insist anyone stop teaching the Believers to take a call.

My brother proceeded to tell me that Mayor Dellums was in the middle of a riot in the street. At that time I didn't know there was rioting. Brother Christopher reminded me that the Honorable Minister Louis Farrakhan asked us to look out for Dellums and help him where we could. So Brother Christopher's next instruction for me was to assemble a team, go downtown, and stand with the Mayor. We could not risk the possibility of Mayor Dellums getting hurt on our watch. Brother Captain and I left with a team of FOI, and we called for others who lived near downtown. We selected a route we thought would get us as near to the Mayor as possible and made our way, unhindered, to City Hall.

When we arrived, we saw Mayor Dellums on the steps of City Hall appealing to an angry crowd of about 250 people. Mayor Dellums declared that he was from West Oakland, and that he understood everyone's anger, but he hoped to deal with concerns peacefully. Mayor Dellums had just done the unimaginable. He walked through a sea of angry rioters, he directed them to follow him to city hall, he appealed to them to gain justice constructively; but, most surprisingly, he ordered the Oakland Police Department to back off, get out of the way, and let him deal with his people. They did; he tried.

Instigators in the crowd, however, cussed at the Mayor and instigated the crowd to boo him down. Mayor Dellums returned to City Hall. He had tears in his eyes fearing that no good would come to our youth that night. When we talked, I assured him that those who cussed him do not know him and that their anger is with the face of government that has not given justice to the poor. To the crowd that night, Mayor Dellums represented the face of the government, so the anger was directed at him. This challenge is one he has yet to recover from. As someone who made his name in Congress as a peace activist, sought freedom for Nelson Mandela, and served as Chairman of the Congressional Committee that managed America's war machine, that night in the twinkling of an eye, he appeared as a sell-out Negro to those young people he was striving to serve. He was in great pain.

Mayor Dellums shared with me that he would instruct OPD to investigate this homicide like it would handle any other homicide in the city of Oakland. He intended to tell the media the same thing, and we turned to face a local news outlet. As soon as he made this statement, however, the closest reporter ordered the camera stopped. "Do you really mean to call this a homicide?" the reporter questioned Mayor Dellums. In response, the Mayor firmly and calmly stated, "Homicide only means by definition that a human being has been killed. It does not declare intention or purpose. A human being has been killed and it should be investigated." That reporter and the network he worked for never did report Mayor Dellums' statement. The media could not bring themselves to report that the murder of Oscar Grant could be considered anything other than an accident or justifiable.

The day after the first night of rioting, Mayor Dellums called me to his office. He wanted me to know that he talked with the District Attorney and they agreed to make a statement to the city. As a matter of public safety, he announced his intention to bring charges against Mehserle and issue a warrant for his arrests. Mayor Dellums asked me would I stand with him in the press conference, and of course I agreed.

In his remarks, Mayor Dellums shared that we should always be concerned about an officer involved shooting because police officers work for the public, are to serve the public, and are paid by the public. The public paid for every gun and every bullet. Therefore, the public had a right to demand transparency in investigations and accountability. He reminded everyone that criminals are held to account in criminal courts.

After insisting that he would not call a press conference to address the public and state his intentions, District Attorney Tom Orloff spoke the very words we had demanded. In front of the press, he declared that he intended to bring charges against Johannes Mehserle.

Oakland, indeed, owes thanks to Mayor Dellums. Many people have had different thoughts about his service as Mayor, but one thing that can never be said is that God did not choose him, a peace-loving activist from the Civil Rights era, to be mayor of Oakland for a time when she desperately needed a calm, loving, voice of reason. I can only imagine what the response may have been from anyone else who may have been in office, who may have felt a need to get tough on crime rather than to pursue justice.

Photo: Victor Muhammad

1. Why did protesters blame Mayor Dellums? How did they view his authority in this situation?
2. Why didn't the reporter want to report the killing of Oscar Grant as a homicide?
3. Why did the District Attorney join Mayor Dellums in addressing the shooting of Oscar Grant?

Mayor Ronald Dellums addresses the January 14, 2009 rally, one day after the arrest of Johannes Mehserle.
Photo: Thomas Hawke

Chapter 7
Activism, Townhall Meetings, and the Caravan for Justice

Muslim and activism goes hand in hand. Since 1930, with the Coming of Master Fard Muhammad, Muslims in North America are noted for personal and collective action. Beginning in Detroit, Master Fard Muhammad actively pursued the suffering masses of Black folks and lovingly courted us. His relationship with us gave rise to 25,000 students and He chose one, Elijah Muhammad, and made him a Messenger to a suffering people in the process of resurrection.

Minister Farrakhan teaches us that resurrection is not just a day; rather, it is a process. This process begins with stimulation of the the self accusing spirit and does not end until we reach oneness with God. This voice of correction within, that many call "conscience" or "super ego", if we obey its direction causes us to do what is right with God. He teaches us that it is in our nature to think right.

Confronted by continued policy decisions that punish and discriminate against our people, an active Muslim is commanded to do something to improve the condition. The principle of jihad, loosely defined as "Holy War" strikes fear into the minds of the wicked out of their fear of being exposed as wicked. Why should any right minded person be frightened of anything holy, unless our thoughts and deeds are ruled by mischief and bloodshed?

Jihad takes on three principle actions. While the media uses fear and propaganda to offer a caricature of Muslim Jihadists, harming the innocent; in truth, jihad is a divine principle for self-improvement found among all people of faith, who have determined that the world we live in is not what it should be, and out of concern and compassion, are willing to make a change.

First, the Believer sees wrong and evil and prays deeply that evil be removed. Secondly, the Believer raises his voice against the existence of evil; that is, to speak against evil. Third, the Believer raises his hand, steps forward on his feet, rolls up his sleeve and goes to work to change evil by stopping it and producing good.

The weekly Townhall meetings found their origins in the inspiration of the Honorable Minister Louis Farrakhan who guided us at the Millions More Movement; the 10th Anniversary of the Million Man March. There, the Minister guided us to construct committees to address the needs of the people called Ministries. Though we were years from the

Millions More Movement, we faced the same conditions that required our people from every walk of life, to unite and organize our response to secure justice against policies that were costing our people life, liberty and the pursuit of happiness.

In San Francisco, with few Blacks remaining in the city population, the Bay View community was confronted with new revelations of designs to further gentrify the city. The Lennar Corporation had broken ground on a housing project sitting on one of the country's most poisonous toxic waste areas. Not surprisingly, this toxic dump Superfund Site sits next to one of the largest low income housing communities in San Francisco.

As the construction workers began leveling the grounds and removing earth, tremendous dust clouds began blowing over the community. Dust clouds were so great that our children, at the Muhammad University of Islam, which sits on the edge of the construction site, had to be brought in from play because of overwhelming dust.

The school was entirely unaware of the dangers contained in the dust. Children played in the dust, breathed it in, and went home and suffered silently thinking they were simply victims in need of skin creams to address rashes, and tissue to deal with nose bleeds.

Chris Carpenter, a worker on the construction site, who was instructed with other workers to stop work and leave due to high levels of dust, asked his employers if the children and school on the hill were informed of the dangers so that they might be equally protected. The answer he was given was to mind his own business. Another work day, dust clouds causing work stoppage, Chris asks again about the children, if this was dangerous for them, and if they have been warned. After being threatened for not minding his own business, Chris punched his work foreman in the nose; got himself arrested; yet local police understood his anger and let him go.

Why was Chris so angry? It is because that dust was not simply dust; it was dust laden with asbestos and other toxins which by law, the community should have been warned and protected from by the regulations and authority of government.

Chris attempted and failed to reach Minister Christopher with warning of the dangers of asbestos exposures for the children and community. He eventually tracked him down and shared the dangers that the children and community had been exposed to asbestos, one of the most toxic substances that workers can be exposed to, which is why the workers were permitted to go home; but, the residents lived without warning absorbing untold deadly toxins.

Brother Christopher began organizing leaders, parents, and eventually those willing politicians to address the community needs. This led to weekly Townhall meetings. The issues of toxic poisoning were so great, that in the absence of willing San Francisco politicians, Brother Christopher asked me if we could share these struggles with the Black Elected Officials and Faith Based Leaders of the East Bay. We did and this produced a tour of the Toxic Triangle and a Public Hearing at Oakland City Hall to address issues of toxic exposure in Black and poor communities.

The Bay Area Nation of Islam began to accept the challenge of addressing political issues facing our cities and communities. Brother Christopher insisted that all of our cities develop a process to involve and include community activists, clergy, politicians and others to address community concerns. In Richmond, Stockton, Sacramento, East Palo Alto, San Francisco and Oakland, Townhall meetings began.

San Francisco activists, fighting with politicians who most glaringly supported a rogue company, Lennar, at any cost went to work organizing. We offered support. Then OPD unleashed a plan to arrests over 50 so-called Acorn gang members in a sting called Operation Nutcracker. Police from 15 cities raided the Acorn housing project, rolled into town in armored vehicles, kicked in doors at 5:00am, tossed flash grenades into homes, and arrested 54 young men.

To add insult to injury, the state Attorney General, Jerry Brown, held a press conference and declared that those arrested had terrorized the community, were urban terrorist, and had been involved in asymmetrical warfare.

We certainly saw the handwriting on the wall. The appeal to stop Black on Black violence has given license to government to use any force, no matter how unjust, and to bring West Oakland into subjection. It did not seem to matter that these arrests could have easily been achieved by good police work, monitoring drug sales, walking the beat, and putting a stop to open air drug markets and the vandalism and petty crime that accompany these lifestyles all over America in the inner cities.

We took exception to this militarization of the community and the criminalization of our youth, justifying for the citizens the need for a military response to social problems. Most youth who are involved in street life are products of broken schools, sometimes of broken families, certainly a broken economy, and broken spirit. This is not a problem that militarization of law enforcement can solve.

Military intervention serves only one purpose; that is, to get and keep land. We discovered that in cities across America, that when a spike in crime encourages heavy increase in law enforcement, gang injunctions, and militarization of police forces, that land is the ultimate aim. The West Oakland community was targeted for redevelopment which results in gentrification. The new residents would come from San Francisco and other areas, not because they love the 'hood,' but because West Oakland is nearer to the downtown financial district of San Francisco than most of the city San Francisco. It is only a 7 minute ride on BART from West Oakland to the financial center of California, San Francisco.

We decided to call Black leadership and challenge Attorney General Brown's attack on the community youth as "urban terrorist" involved in "asymmetrical warfare". At a press conference held just across the street from the housing project; three groups appeared at the press conference; the police, concerned residents and us. Residents from Acorn came curiously wondering, "Who are these leaders that are defending us?" Unfortunately, the silence of Black leadership on many issues affecting our lives has been deafening.

As we witnessed the press coverage of young Black men, depicted as the root cause of our community suffering, and wearing labels better suited for so-called terrorists in the war on Iraq, we knew someone needed to stand in the gap to offer protection for our young who are too often the targets of unjust law enforcement measures. We understood that once our young are feared as terrorists, then the process of education is secondary to the process of incarceration. The Million Man March was inspired by the plans of government to target Black youth. We felt it our duty to protect the young men that many of us marched to defend in 1995.

This gave birth to the concept of hosting weekly Townhall meetings. We worked to produce a political force to command the respect of government. At the Millions More Movement, the Honorable Minister Louis Farrakhan said that we do not need a third political party, but a third political force. The Townhall would become the place for that force to meet and develop political strategies.

On January 3, just two days after Oscar was killed, we hosted a men only Townhall at Olivet. Reverend Gordon Humphreys, though generally soft spoken and mild mannered graciously permitted us the use of his church. Olivet had become the most accessible church for these kinds of community affairs. Pastor Humphrey, a man whose father pastored in Chicago and sat with the Most Honorable Elijah Muhammad, had a heart and desire to see our people, regardless of faith tradition and denomination, to unite. He had been making himself and his church readily available for the needs of the community.

At that meeting, we addressed the increased criminalization, the effects of implementation of the three strikes law, mass incarceration, privatizing of prisons and gentrification of our community. Men gathered from all over the Bay Area. While facilitating the meeting, I asked the men if any knew of the killing on BART on New Years. Few had knowledge, even fewer had facts. Later that night, the video went out on YouTube and KTVU and the Journey for Justice would be inspired.

Immediately, Oakland began a weekly Townhall to address the murder of Oscar Grant. Supporters came from all over the Bay area participating in the weekly meeting to learn the conditions and plan solutions. In addition to the murder of Oscar, we regularly discussed injustice in environment, education, law enforcement policy and poverty.

A leadership team emerged to plan our meetings and strategize solutions. Minister Christopher recommended that we develop a leadership team to respond to community needs. His suggestion was to organize a nervous system to feel the pains of, and produce solutions to, the suffering of our community. The murder of Oscar Grant demanded an organized response.

I am grateful for the support of the Oakland team of Pastors, Activists, and the family and friends of Oscar Grant. Pastor Gordon Humphreys, who had made his church readily available for any community need and has given moral support to every challenge. Pastor

Zachery Carey, whose strong stands with us, was so impressive that many thought he must be a "Muslim" minister. Pastor Dion Evans, whose evangelical work and schedule may have deterred him from full participation, but his early organizing efforts are clearly noted by me, Rev. Daniel Buford, who came to us in the Toxic Triangle struggle, but like Pastor Carey, his presentation was so strong, that he seemed to enjoy standing and speaking like the Honorable Minister Louis Farrakhan. Rev. Lawrence Van Hook, whose rise into position over a Pastors Union may have deterred him, but who can forget his decry, "I am Oscar Grant." Others would join onto the team as the Townhall progressed; including, political legend Wilson Riles, Black Caucus of Oakland President who drafted Mayor Dellums, Geoffrey Pete, San Francisco State student activist and Pastor, Sister Ramona Tascoe, and others who stood up as the journey for justice continued.

With hundreds of concerned citizens involved, the Townhall began to make demands. With other organizations such as BAMN (By Any Means Necessary), the General Assembly for Justice for Oscar Grant, the New Years Committee for Justice for Oscar Grant, and the Oscar Grant family, the pursuit for justice was on.

We demanded that the DA resign, retire, or face a recall. After weeks of failing to get our application for recall accepted by the County Registrar; DA Tom Orloff retired.

With legal analyst bringing us weekly updates on the merits of the case; at the Townhall we were left well able to challenge the district attorney strategy and to challenge the defense attorney's tactics. Oakland's rich history of fighting police brutality provided a firm foundation for understanding the issues.

These meetings equipped us with knowledge and support to challenge BART and legislature to bring changes in public policy. BART police chief Gee eventually retired under the unrelenting pressure of activists on the BART Board to fire him. BART developed a committee to develop a citizen review process which passed unanimously through its Board vote; the state legislature, though weakening the original document, passed Assembly Bill 1586 (The BART Accountability Act – Assemblyman Sandre' Swanson) into law and BART should have oversight in place by January 2011. BART fired the two cops whose actions the night of Oscar's murder precipitated the killing; that is Anthony Pirone, who called Oscar a "bitch ass nigger" and his partner, Marisol Domenici, who declared such fear that she knew she would have to shoot someone on the platform that night. All of these things represent firsts in the history of California.

On February 17, 2009, the Honorable Minister Louis Farrakhan traveled to the Bay Area to support, acknowledge, and bless the efforts launched in San Francisco in the fight for justice against Lennar. The murder of Oscar Grant demanded the attention of us all. As a result, the Ministers planned visit to support the efforts for justice in San Francisco was refocused on Oakland and the murder of Oscar Grant.

The Minister took time to meet with community leaders, activists and elected officials at True Vine Church, where we were hosted by Reverend Zachery Carey. He held private meetings, battled fatigue and overcame health challenges. As we discussed the proposed visit to Olivet for an evening Townhall; he insisted that regardless of difficulty with his health, that he was coming to the Townhall. We were greatly blessed to receive inspiration, guidance, love and support at a packed Olivet Church.

He wisely reminded us that while we cry out for justice whenever one of our people are assassinated by police; that we must also cry out whenever we lose our lives to the senseless killing of one another. One of the leading causes of death in the Black community is homicide and the overwhelming number of homicide victims, were killed by another Black man.

We knew this journey for justice did not begin, nor would it end with Oscar Grant. So we organized people all over Northern California to address the many policy issues that afflict the Black, the Brown, and the poor. We galvanized the support of Townhall meetings in eight cities (San Francisco, Richmond, Antioch, East Palo Alto, Stockton, Modesto, Pittsburg and Oakland), ordered buses and took cars and made our way to Sacramento on the Caravan for Justice.

The first Caravan for Justice arrived in Sacramento on February 19, 2009 to find a welcome party of horse mounted police, rooftop police snipers, and a heavy dose of law enforcement crowd control apparatus. The Legislature was in special session all night long and just agreed on an overdue budget.

With about 1000 activists, from 8 cities, Black, Brown, Red, Yellow and White, young and old, united on a platform of justice for the oppressed, the Caravan and the spirit it projected compelled

48

Assemblyman Sandre Swanson and Assemblyman Joe Coto, chairman of the Latino Legislative Caucus to emerge from all night budget hearings and join us at the Caravan.

After all speakers had delivered their messages; it was clear that justice for Oscar Grant was what the state police feared most. His killing had taken root in the hearts of activists, many of whom had never seen a BART train, had never met Oscar Grant and his family, but insisted that after hearing his story and watching on television, that justice must be served.

Brother Christopher insisted that we enter the state capitol building and take a tour. You could see the fear and concern in the eyes of state police. As we lined up to enter, we couldn't help but wonder what it was like for a dozen Black Panthers in May of 1967, to walk into the Capitol with guns. Without firing a shot, the Panthers sent a shot heard around the world.

On this day, without carrying a weapon; only the weapon of unity, a shot was heard by the legislature that the people have organized to demand change. The people, united throughout the Bay area, were in the house to demand change. Once inside the Capitol building; we stopped our tour, gathered in the rotunda, and announced our intention and right to demand and petition the government, if it is ours, to bring about policy changes that would relieve us of the pain and suffering of unjust policies that do not respect nor protect the rights of the poor, the Black and brown, from criminalization, incarceration, exposure to deadly toxins, and constant barrage of police brutality.

The Caravans would return to Sacramento on three occasions. Each time with the support and assistance of State Black Caucus chair, Assemblyman Sandre' Swanson and his staff, who acknowledged our delegation as hundreds of us entered the chambers as the legislature deliberated policy. Each Caravan delivered greater support with activist traveling from Southern California, the Central Valley and the Bay Area to unite in our demands for justice. Caravan for Justice 4 may be coming soon since justice still stands afar.

Oakland Townhall at Olivet hears from BART leaders. On the first row, right side, are Director Lynette Sweet, General Manager Dorothy Dugger, Director Carol Ward-Allen, and Director Bob Franklin.
Photo: Reginald James

1. "Organization is more important than truth, because an organized lie has more power than disorganized truth." Minister Louis Farrakhan
   Do you agree with this axiom? Explain your answer.
2. What are some actions taken by Bay Area activist to secure justice?
3. Why did activist bring their demands to the BART Board of Directors?
4. Why did activist take their demands to Sacramento?
5. How were demands made by the public responded to the murder of Oscar Grant?
6. Do you think D.A. Orloff would have charged Johannes Mehserle with murder without public demand?
7. What are some of the issues that activists raised in the Caravan for Justice?

The Honorable Minister Louis Farrakhan historic visit on February 17, 2009
Photo: Reginald James

Chapter 8
Oakland on Trial

Photo: Victor Muhammad

The murder of Oscar Grant produced a unique challenge for Oakland's unique political structure. Oakland is the political home of legendary Congressman, now Mayor Ronald V. Dellums. Oakland is the district of Congressional Black Caucus chairperson, Congressperson Barbara Lee. Oakland is the district of State Black Caucus leader, Assemblyman Sandre Swanson. Oakland is the home base for the Black Panther Party. Oakland appears to be the last predominantly Black city in the West coast and has enough Black elected officials to make a difference.

It was Oakland's Black elected officials to whom we reached to learn what could be done to bring justice in the murder of Oscar Grant. Fortunately, we have an organization, led by County Supervisor Keith Carson, designed to unite and organize the efforts of Black elected officials. Unfortunately, unity and purpose had been difficult to achieve. The murder of Oscar Grant demanded leadership. Since the people have elected our representatives into many offices; it was clear to us that power in political offices means nothing if the politician is not willing or able to stand for justice.

No one could watch the video of Oscar Grant and not be compelled to demand justice. Black elected officials are uniquely placed to realize our demands. It serves us no purpose to have Black elected officials if they will not stand up for Black people. So we reached out and touched as many as we could with our concerns.

What we discovered was, most were as concerned as we were, but did not know how to bring the changes desired. Most of our current elected officials were children in the 60's radical era, saw the rise and fall of the Panther Party, and chose their careers in public service hoping to serve the needs of our people. Surely, most discovered that the wheels of change for the needs of our own seem to grind exceedingly slow. It's as though we were asked to 'hurry up and wait.'

To their credit, every Black elected official that we asked to meet and share our concerns, heard us out, generally agreed, and many made themselves available to the community. Councilperson Desley is famous for protesting with activists as if handcuffed and crying out, "Don't shoot." She then spoke out in BART Board and public meetings and challenged anybody unwilling to recognize the pain of watching the execution of Oscar Grant. Supervisor Carson joined Ms. Brooks and challenged the BART Board to do the same.

Perhaps for the first time, protesters came from every walk of life. A state commissioner of public utilities arrived at one BART Board meeting and complained how his teenage daughter was a victim of BART police racial profiling. A new organization drew together activist who were Black and White, nationalist and socialist, even some anarchist and called themselves CAPE (Coalition against Police Execution), led by Dereca Blackman and were the principle organizers of the January 7, 2009 rally at Fruitvale BART station. Members of churches and mosques attended most public events; but special thanks must go to the members of the Nation of Islam, who have made the sacrifices needed to drive the Journey for Justice.

As activist awaited the preliminary trial for Johannes Mehserle, the city was on edge as we pondered if the District Attorney would do the right thing and prosecute Mehserle to the fullest extent of the law; a tragic incident derailed the proposed court dates. Lovelle Mixon, a young Black man driving in East Oakland, on being stopped by two motorcycle officers for an alleged routine traffic stop, opened fire and killed two officers. He fled on foot into the home of his sister about a block away. As he hid and took cover inside, OPD officers rushed the door, tossed in a flash grenade, and opened fire. Mixon returned fire, killing 2 more police before succumbing to a hail of bullets.

Police throughout the state mourned the loss of 4 police officers in one incident. OPD and its neighboring forces were in no mood to hear about Oscar Grant. Some activists, challenging police actions in the Mixon shooting captured video of the rage in the hearts of some Black youth at the police and recording many declaring this shooting was payback for Oscar Grant. This is really a fearless generation.

The Alameda County Courts were advised by the Sheriff's department to delay the preliminary trial of Oscar because of its fear of how police and public would conflict in light of the passion of those wanting justice for the murder of Oscar; but even more importantly, the passion and anger of police directed at protesters they believe to be insensitive to their needs after the killing of four cops.

I attended the funeral of the 4 officers held at the Oakland Arena and Coliseum. It was a sight to see. Police arrived in full regalia. There were SWAT teams, Armored Personnel vehicles on display, more than 50,000 police and supporters; but conspicuously absent from the program was Mayor Dellums.

54

The same Mayor who gave his state of the city address and spoke to the issue of Oscar Grant, declared his willingness to have OPD take over the investigation from BART, reduced the overtime pay schedule that OPD union had secured for its officers; breaking down the city budget to nothing, and demanding the OPD accept community policing as its standard operating procedure. Mayor Dellums, though the city of Oakland was paying thousands of dollars into this funeral, was not invited to speak. Would this have happened if Mayor Dellums were a white mayor?

Once the preliminary hearings began, it was clear that the people wanted justice for Oscar. Activist waited at 6:00am each day of the hearings to attempt to secure seats. Jack Bryson, whose sons were with Oscar the night he was killed would always be among the first to arrive. Sister Beatrice X, with or without transportation, arrived faithfully to court each day. The Grant family, Wanda, Cephus, and friends arrived each day to a warm activists welcome. Each day, the press was guaranteed most of the seats in the court.

Protests were held nearly every day as the hearings proceeded. The Sheriffs had to implement special procedures to insure that court was not overfilled. The Sherriff's Department was so concerned that when we pointed out for the sheriff that Oscars friends were being targeted for removal from court by bailiffs, the sheriff told us the this trial was the worst thing ever to happen in the court and he could not wait for this to be over. He pointed out of his window at less than a dozen protesters and declared this to be his biggest problem.

I am sure Tony Coleman, Yvette Falarca, Dave ID, Cat and others never knew how much fear their presence was to the sheriffs; but this simply proves that police have a mind and culture of their own. These protesters never posed a threat to police. In fact, police posed a threat to the protesters. I watched a motorcycle officer, in an attempt to force marchers off the street and onto a sidewalk, nearly run over a marcher with his motorcycle. When the young man responded by defending his body from hit and run, he was quickly arrested. Tensions were high between police and protesters, but, most tension was found in officer responses to the freedom of speech.

1. Why did Oakland police officers deny Mayor Dellums a role in the funeral of the 4 officers killed by Lovelle Mixon?

2. What impact did the Mixon incident have on the trial of Johannes Mehserle?

3. How did Sherriff Ahern feel about hosting the Mehserle trial at the Alameda County Courthouse?

4. How did Black elected officials respond to the murder of Oscar Grant? How did these elected officials respond to community activism?

OPD prepares for riots. Photo: Gene Hazzard

Chapter 9
Preliminary Hearing, Change of Venue, Rodney King and Oscar Grant

Photo: Gene Hazzard

Once in court, we were pleased to see a Black judge, Don Clay. The preliminary hearing, which often lasts a couple of days, dragged on about 2 $1/2$ weeks. This was a result of the defense attorney for Mehserle desire to provide an overwhelming amount of expert testimony.

It was here that we were able to see, daily, Johannes Mehserle. It was here that we were able to hear what his defense would be. It was here that we would see and hear multiple videos and the testimony of the videographers. It was here that we would see and hear the man who BART police claimed that Oscar wrestled or fought with. Perhaps the most significant thing we saw and heard was the responses of BART police and the levels to which they were willing to go to cover the crime of Mehserle.

Not a single BART cop testified to hearing a gunshot: amazing. All of them testified to hearing a "strange sounding taser", a "loud sound", and a "loud noise."

The most memorable parts of testimony came from Jamil Dewar, Officer Tony Pirone and Officer Marisol Domenici.

Jamil, the 15 year old friend of Oscar who witnessed the shooting and captured part of the night on his cell phone camera brought the house to tears and laughter. It was clear that he was a little nervous, but his fighting spirit for justice was clear. He intended to defend his friend and testify for justice. When questioned about the use of the n-word by defense attorneys, seeking to desensitize the judge to the fact that Pirone called Oscar by the n-word; Jamil gave attorney Rains a lesson in Black street vernacular. When asked if he used the word nigger; Jamil declared, no I said nigga. Nigger is used by white racist like Pirone; but nigga is a term I used for a friend. He left attorney Rains, for the first time in this trial.

Marisol Domenici will be forever remembered for her expression of fear that almost sounded comedic. I thought to myself as she testified, "She could not really believe what she is saying." She sounded like the BART police version of Sarah Palin. She testified to running onto the BART platform through a riotous crowd of hundreds of people. She testified that she ran fearfully to the aid of her partner Pirone, who had detained Oscar's friends on the platform. She said she was so concerned that she knew that she would have to shoot someone.

Her words sounded so real, so sincere to her; until video evidence contradicted her every word. The video showed that she never ran past hundreds. The video showed she never ran past dozens. The video showed that she never ran past a single person on the way to aid Officer Pirone on the platform. It took slow motion, repeated viewing of the video by the prosecutor, to show her to either have been blinded by fear or outwardly lying. The lie was so tremendous and shocking that Judge Clay had to ask a question. He asked, "Just who were you going to shoot when you got up there?"

Anthony Pirone walked into court like a proud marine, prepared to tell us how he had just taken Iwo Jima. He was clearly a proud and arrogant man. He boasted of his fighting skills, physical build, and the respect shown to him by his fellow officers. Most significantly, he boasted how he manhandled Michael Greer, Oscar's friend whom he snatched off the train and forced to the ground.

Mr. Pirone was confronted by continuous video evidence that contradicted his testimony. The prosecutor asked him if he had used any racial epithets to Oscar Grant. Reminiscent of the O.J. Simpson trial testimony of Mark Furman, Pirone denied ever using such foul and racially offensive language. However, the prosecution presented video evidence with audio recording which captured Pirone shouting at Oscar Grant, "Bitch Ass Nigger". He shouted the phrase twice just seconds before Oscar was killed. This was shown to him just after he denied ever saying what video evidence revealed. His lie was uncovered. He couldn't cover it up. He even alleged that Oscar called him a "bitch ass nigger" first and that he was so shocked, that he must have returning the comment out of shock.

In the face of video evidence, each BART cop was proven to lie in their reports. In fact, some modified their story only after the video experts, hired by lawyers told them how to interpret the actions seen on tape. Pirone went so far as to accuse Oscar of trying to kick him twice. Nowhere in his initial report does he suggest that Oscar ever touched him, but when his lawyer told him Oscar may have done this, Pirone was left trying to explain a kick that never happened. Another lie by BART police officer was exposed.

By the time he left the witness stand, the proud marine had his big ego deflated. He was publically embarrassed, but he surely knew, this trial was far from over, and would have to testify again.

At the conclusion of the preliminary hearing, Judge Clay made a profound declaration in binding this case over for trial. He declared, "I have no doubt in my mind that Johannes Mehserle intended to use a gun and not a taser." He then scheduled Mehserle for the next phase of hearings. It was time to set a trial date.

Confronted with a pending trial, Johannes Mehserle instructed his attorney to file a motion to change the venue. A new judge, Morris Jacobson, would carry the case. Attorney Rains brought in jury experts to testify to the impact of the case on a potential jury. His case in chief declared that since elected officials, Black clergy leaders, and Black activists have called the murder of Oscar Grant an execution that Alameda County could not have a fair trial. Attorney Rains brought to court thousands of newspaper articles and asserted that the area had been saturated with news carrying the views of respected political and community leaders. He argued that the pressure to find a guilty verdict was too great to insure a jury could be fair to his client, Johannes Mehserle.

Central to his argument were the alleged views of Blacks in the jury pool and the fact that factors in history make it impossible for a white cop to be tried fairly in the town that gave birth to the Black Panthers and whose Muslims were influencing and driving the movement for justice. He even went so far as to falsely accuse the Muslims of having a history of violence with police and involvement in Bay Area crimes. Certainly, we were outraged with his filing and wanted to challenge him for defamation, only to learn that in California, lawyers can lie in court records and not be compelled to answer the lie.

As the trial moved near conclusion, Attorney Rains walked into court near his closing statements armed with the local newspaper. After his argument that this case received more press attention than any case in history; he had already brought into court a mountain of newspapers as his evidence. There were hundreds of newspapers stacked on a table most of the hearing. On the first day of the venue hearing, activists held a press conference outside the Alameda County Courthouse, then entered and witnessed the days court procedure.

The next morning, to my surprise, it was brought to my attention that my picture was on the cover of the local paper, the Oakland Tribune. I was shocked by this because this rally did not result in any violence against people or property. We didn't stay long and did not answer any questions. More intriguing to me was the fact that of all the media we have dealt with in Oakland, the Tribune never seemed interested in reporting activity involving local Black activist. Why would the Tribune put our event on its cover? This never happened before.

The Oakland Tribune has never proven itself to be a friend to the Black community in its coverage of events. I will never forget the 1995 visit to Oakland of the Honorable Minister Louis Farrakhan. We were blessed to be selected by him as a city he would visit to promote the Million Man March. With only a couple of weeks preparation, we hosted the Minister and he addressed community leaders, held a press conference and that evening addressed about 5000 people in support of the Million Man March.

The next morning I picked up the newspaper, believing the press conference and event would make the news. To my surprise, the Tribune covered that the Minister was in town, however, there was not a single quote from his speech and press conference. Most significantly missing in action was Chauncey Bailey, the Oakland Tribune reporter that covered local black activism. Every effort needing positive coverage would have been covered by Chauncey Bailey.

The Oakland Tribune did not send Chauncey Bailey to the press conference. The Oakland Tribune did not send Chauncey Bailey to cover the rally of 5000 supporters. Its coverage was weak, inaccurate and ineffective. At best, it rehashed old false allegations of alleged anti-Semitism against Minister Farrakhan.

Attorney Rains came to court with the daily paper in his hand and declared, "You see, your honor, this is the kind of press attention that makes it impossible for my client to get a fair trial here." On the cover of that paper was me, standing before protestors holding signs declaring, "Jail Racist Killer Cops," "I am Oscar Grant," and "The Whole Damn System is Guilty."

Judge Jacobson asked if this was coverage of yesterday's rally at lunchtime. Rains answered yes. Jacobson said that crowd of about 100 people in front. Rains said yes. Jacobson said, you mean that crowd I walked through to get my sandwich. In other words, our rally certainly posed no threat to the Judge, but Rains entered into evidence the coverage of our rally as proof of the difficulty of trying this case fairly in Alameda County.

Oakland is about 30% black in population; Alameda County is only 14% Black. Jury pools called in Alameda County are rarely predominantly Black and in truth, many in the Black community have chosen to avoid jury duty. As a result, we rarely are tried by a jury of our peers; rather, a jury of other than our peers.

Judge Jacobson accepted the requests from defense attorneys to move the trial out of Alameda County. After additional research and hearings, it was determined that the only reasonable options for a site would be San Diego and Los Angeles.

San Diego, a wealthy and conservative city, known as a Republican base in California, was not seen as a good option for us. It was the area that celebrates former President Ronald Reagan. Selection of San Diego would have been received as an open attack on justice.

Judge Jacobson eventually selected Los Angeles. After analysis of costs of trial, ability to meet public safety demands and handle press attention, Los Angeles became the logical choice. Moving to San Diego would have required tremendous amounts of money because it was not equipped to handle the security, public and press demands, with burdening the already tight court and county budget.

Los Angeles was the chosen city. It was home of the Rodney King Case that was often referred to in the motion change arguments. The politics and controversy of that case established legal precedent currently used for venue change motions. Los Angeles is certainly well aware of the pain of police brutality.

We wanted to stay home and support the demand for justice, but if we must travel, Los Angeles appeared to be the best available option to the Grant family in its pursuit of Justice for the Murder of Oscar Grant.

1. Who is qualified to serve on a jury?
2. What happened in the Rodney King trial? Why did this case set legal precedents?
3. What settlement did Rodney King resolve with the City of Los Angeles?
4. After the police who beat Rodney King were acquitted in State court, how did the Federal court respond?
5. Why did defense attorneys refer to the influence of the Black Panther Party and the Muslims on public protests?
6. Why did Judge Don Clay order this case over for trial?

Local 10, Dock Workers Union October 23, 2010 rally for Oscar Grant. The Port of Oakland was shut down. Elaine Brown, former Black Panther Party chair speaks. Union activists Jack Heyman and Jack Bryson in background.
Photo: Gene Hazzard

Chapter 10
Trial

Photo: Gene Hazzard

From the first day of trial and hearings in Los Angeles, it was clear that getting justice there would require the same kind of fight as it did in Oakland. The Los Angeles Coalition for Justice for Oscar Grant and other community activists greeted the Oakland delegation warmly. Dozens travelled in pursuit of justice as Oscar's family made their way from Northern to Southern California. There we were, in Los Angeles, unaware of what to expect, and yet upon arrival to the court, we felt at home among the local activists.

The signs of protesters demanding justice seen at the Oakland Courthouse had been reproduced and carried to Los Angeles. Banners declaring, "I am Oscar Grant", "Grant Justice", and "The Whole Damn System is Guilty" were posted on walls, carried in protesters hands and distributed on handbills. The support of Los Angeles and its united effort with Bay Area activists was clear. The Oscar Grant case had come to town, activism and all.

The media met activists to cover their concerns, but most significant was the activists' willingness to permit the Bay Area spokespersons to take the lead. Our group from Oakland just met the organizers in Los Angeles like Aidge Patterson, but once the group from L.A. decided to engage press, they humbly conceded that this movement was best represented by our coalition from Oakland. It was a seamless transition. The community from L.A. supported our cry for justice, and it looked like Oakland activists had just taken over the Los Angeles County Courthouse.

Johannes Mehserle was discretely escorted into the court daily to avoid activists, who gathered everyday at 8:00 A.M. to demonstrate. Activists waited daily for us to emerge from court and entertained the press with rallies until we agreed to address the media. Usually, that meant Cephus Johnson and Attorney John Burris, but Wanda was clearly appreciative of the support and one day chose to address the press.

Judge Robert Perry was neither impressed nor pleased with the activism. On the first day of trial, while hearing motions and setting court dates, Judge Perry acknowledged the press's desire to record court proceedings and rejected the motion. It was clear that Los Angeles courts were afraid to have another OJ Simpson case where the Judge, jury and attorneys all appeared to be affected by the constant press attention. When Judge Perry addressed schedules, he acknowledged the protests outside the court. He sternly made clear that he would tolerate no outbursts by protesters in court. He made it clear that no political expressions like T-Shirts bearing Oscar's face, banners and handbills were permitted in court. The most controversial thing he stated was that he intended to have a fair trial here in Los Angeles. He reiterated that it was the right of the accused to have a fair trial, and he spoke to the fact that it was the protestors' actions which contributed to the venue change to Los Angeles in the first place. He went further to say that we would have a fair trial there, even if it took five years. He was willing to wait out the anger of protesters.

Justice delayed is justice denied. The family left court feeling as if the judge was offended by the level of support the people showed them. Why would a judge in a murder case be more concerned about 100 to 200 protesters than he would be of the killing of Oscar Grant?

Soon, the Judge would hear arguments about jury selection and its process. Many experts shared with us that this would be a critical part of this trial. Attorneys reviewed the judges' recommendations, offered their own views, and proceeded to bring in potential jurors in a systematic way.

Unfortunately, Judge Perry, the Prosecution and the Defense agreed to a juror questionnaire that provided questions that would exclude most Black people from participation. Answer these questions for yourself:

- Do you think police sometimes lie?

- Have you ever been a victim of racial profiling?

- Do you think police always tell the truth?

- Do you know anyone that has ever been abused by police?

By the time they finished providing jurors with these questions, every Black potential juror had been thanked and excused from service. The prosecution let this slide without challenge. This left us to wonder if the prosecution was indeed willing to fight for justice for the murder of Oscar Grant.

Opening arguments would proceed in the trial without a Black juror. On June 10, prosecutor David Stein and defense attorney Michael Rains presented the basis of their arguments.

Mr. Stein painted a picture of a group of police out of control, who, when confronted with evidence, began to change their story to fit the known evidence. He painted a picture of Mehserle as an officer who consciously and carefully aimed his firearm at an unarmed, defenseless man, and murdered him. The prosecutor argued for second degree murder; not manslaughter.

The defense attorney presented a case based on testimony from witnesses he felt would prove that Mehserle was a victim of poor training and weapons confusion under stress. He further argued that Oscar Grant and his friends vehemently resisted arrest leading to the escalation of force by law enforcement. Judge Perry even permitted Rains to introduce an incident that Oscar had been involved in when he was tasered by police at the age of 17. It was an event, he argued, that caused Oscar to fear being tasered and had a history of resisting arrest.

For weeks, the trial dragged on. The prosecution brought on witnesses who taped the scene, police experts on use of force rules and training, and other witnesses to the killing. He presented a decent argument, but not a compelling case. We were hopeful because we believed that Mehserle was guilty. Unfortunately, the burden of proof was on the prosecution, and we were not sure what the prosecutor really believed.

The defense attorneys brought on so-called experts in policing, one after another. All of these experts were current or former police officers, weapons trainers, or video experts. All seemed to be well paid. These were professional witnesses who supported police conduct.

The prosecution questioned them about their relationship with police departments and their salary for giving testimony. One witness earned more than $50,000 for bringing testimony supporting Rains contentions. The video expert was the first to come unto the defense team because they knew this case was built on video evidence. Lastly, he relied on police testimony to assert that Oscar was resisting arrest at the time he was shot.

The testimony of Oscar's friends, Jackie Bryson, Jamil Dewar and Carlos Reyes brought the courtroom to tears. The passion and spirit of these young men and their love for Oscar was evident. Their testimony left Judge Perry moved and scrambling for order, and forced him to declare a recess to bring calm to the courtroom.

As each nervously took the stand, it was clear their nerves eased, especially when challenged by defense attorney, Michael Rains. For them, Rains represented the enemy. The more Rains pushed, the more they pushed back. Each witness brought testimony to an event so painful for them that they had only seen the video tape in court. Can you imagine a teenager whose image is on TV every day for several months but never once watches? This was too painful for them.

These young men are the unspoken heroes of this case. Jackie Bryson, Nigel Bryson, Carlos Reyes, Michael Greer, Jontue Caldwell, and others are the proud, brave, angry and frightened young men who witnessed an execution of their best friend. They loved Oscar. He seemed to be part of the glue that kept them together. I was moved to tears with them as they recounted the murder of Oscar and how they were treated by BART police. These young men were terrorized and abused. They came prepared to fight terrorists with the testimony of truth.

Jackie Bryson, Oscar's friend, was seen on tape being escorted away from the shooting scene in handcuffs, screaming in anguish. He was taken to BART police station, charged with no crime, held for 6 hours in handcuffs, mocked by Anthony Pirone and others, and deceived by BART interrogators without a lawyer and witnesses. He was further tortured by his being kept from the knowledge of Oscar's condition. He did not know if Oscar was dead or alive.

They exploited his pain and lack of knowledge of his civil rights. He did not know how to assert his right to an attorney. He did not know how to assert his right to remain silent. He spoke words out of fear and distrust of police and when asked why his words appear different, he asserted that he had just watched them murder his friend for nothing, that he didn't know what they would do to him. He broke down and cried. His family broke down and cried. Jurors cried, and Judge Perry cleared the court.

Jamil Dewar, a 15 year-old young man, who witnessed the shooting and captured footage on his cell phone and brought even greater passion to the courtroom. As attorney Rains questioned him, it was clear Jamil had a problem with Rains. The moment of greatest tension came when Jamil was asked to view his own video of the crime. While the tape rolled, with Jamil looking into the face of the killer of his friend and big brother, with the jury and audience watching the screen, Jamil began to openly sob. He broke down on the witness stand. His pain and emotion was so profound that Judge Perry again, had to order a recess as Jamil's mother rushed to the witness stand to comfort her son.

After the break, Attorney Rains attempted to challenge Jamil about his tears. He wickedly suggested that Jamil was faking or acting. His challenge was met by Jamil's sincerity and sternness as he shared that he has never looked at these tapes. Jamil seemed to make his mark on the hearts of the jurors and those of us witnessing from the audience. He was real. It was too painful for him to view this tape and talk about it in open court. Who would want to review the tape of his friend's murder?

With the pending testimony of Marisol Domenici and Anthony Pirone, we all knew that the high emotions of this court were far from over. Oscar's friends were young and strong. They were passionate and pained, but they did not know whether they could trust the system to render justice. They did not know if the efforts of activists would bear fruit and deliver justice.

Angry as each of these young men were, they arrived in court with dignity, testified with truth and represented themselves well. I was impressed by their manners, their disposition, and their love for friend and family. Each of them came to court dressed in shirt and tie. They negated, in their personage, the image of a group of gang banging thugs whose behavior warranted the behavior of Anthony Pirone and Johannes Mehserle.

Imagine their thoughts coming to court each day and finding that law enforcement surrounded Mehserle, not to prevent a prisoner from escape, but to instead protect Mehserle from the people who desire justice. The security of the court remained on protecting Mehserle and his family. The Grant family received no cooperative attention or security from the court. It was protected by its faith in God and support of the community.

Perhaps the most notable thing spoken by police witnesses came from testimony of Anthony Pirone. As he described the events leading to the murder of Oscar Grant, he asserted his complete shock of Mehserle's stand and shooting of Oscar because, according to Pirone, he already had Oscar under control. There was no need to use a weapon.

For all of his glaring faults, Pirone, the man who twice called Oscar a "bitch ass nigger," he was honest enough to reveal that Oscar was not resisting to the point that required any use of a weapon.

This trial contained so many elements and so much information, that I would advise any who desire further detail to search out the court transcripts. They are a matter of public record. Unlike the OJ Simpson case, this significant trial was not televised. To understand the passion of those who witnessed the evidence and argument, one must really put oneself into the details. After review of the evidence, you will see what the jury saw, and you will surely conclude as the jury did that Johannes Mehserle is guilty.

The community challenges BART with righteous indignation.
Photo: Victor Muhammad

Note: Not a single police officer admitted to hearing a gunshot, including Johannes Mehserle.

1. What is perjury?

2. How much can an attorney pay an "expert witness"? Is there any legal standard? Should there be a standard to insure witnesses do not speak for money rather than for justice?

3. Why did the friends of Oscar Grant distrust BART police and Mehserle's attorney?

4. In the O.J. Simpson case, much attention was given to an officer who used the n-word and denied it in testimony. How significant was it that Officer Pirone called Oscar by such an offensive term?

5. Is it important for Blacks to serve jury duty? How important is jury selection during trials? Answer the juror questions found on page 63 in the chapter. Do you think that you would have been challenged or accepted by the lawyers in the jury selection process?

6. Why didn't Judge Perry permit the press to bring cameras into court?

7. Does the testimony of an expert video witness have greater validity than the jurors' ability to interpret a video?

8. Does the testimony of a police officer have greater validity than the testimony of a citizen?

Chapter 11
The Verdict

Photo: Gene Hazzard

Since January 1, 2009, the family of Oscar Grant has been in pursuit of justice. When the community learned of the murder of Oscar with the January 3rd video release, we joined the family in this pursuit. On July 8, 2010, the primary objective of our pursuit would be realized. Will the jury bring back a guilty verdict? Will the jury see what we have all seen?

Months of time, talent and energy had gone into mourning, meetings, galvanizing and organizing the community to bring justice for the murder of Oscar Grant. On July 8, 2010, we would receive in a Los Angeles courtroom an answer from a jury to confirm our views or to reject them. This moment was tense for all involved.

The City of Oakland was on high alert for rioting. Law enforcement made public demonstrations and exercises of crowd control techniques. Bay area Police departments, sheriff departments, and federal agents practiced joint operations and prepared for the worse. Governor Schwarzenegger put the National Guard on alert.

In the days nearing the verdict, I received calls from Congressperson Lee, Mayor Dellums, and OPD Chief Batts because all were concerned with the reaction to a negative verdict.

The city was so alarmed that it appeared to be looking under every rock for rioters and those who inspire riots. Public pronouncements were made saying that most of those involved in riotous behavior were anarchists and came from other cities.

I was asked on KPFA radio my thought about persons coming to Oakland to protest who came from out of town. I reminded the listening audience that the Reverend Martin Luther King Jr. was not from Montgomery, Alabama; therefore, be careful suggesting that anyone from out of town was evil and plotting to destroy Oakland. Dr. King stated that injustice anywhere was a threat to justice everywhere. Rev. King was even accused by religious leadership for being an out of town, troublemaker. This is what prompted the famed "Letter from a Birmingham Jail." If we want peace; we should bring justice.

Prior to the verdict announcement, the jury had very little time for deliberations. One juror had a medical appointment, causing the jury to delay meeting. Another juror had to travel, a fact known by the court before this juror was selected, yet in Judge Perry's rush to conclude this controversial case, this juror was permitted to remain. However, when his travel date arrived, the jury had to accept an alternate juror and begin deliberating again.

On July 8, with a new juror in position, set in place on the afternoon of July 7, we were prepared to wait for days, or even weeks, for a verdict. We all went to lunch after meeting with attorney Burris. I went to an office supply to buy a pad and to my mother's home. Wanda had fallen ill from the stress of trial and had to be taken to the hospital a few days before. We arranged for her to visit a spa owned by Sister Rita Muhammad with Sister Beatrice, to give her a chance to relax. Cephus went his own direction. Each of us believing this wait would be days.

As soon as I arrived to my mother's home and removed my suit, I received a call. The verdict was in. I was shocked, astounded, and nearly speechless. I actually bought a pad to write my thoughts in preparation for a verdict. After receiving guidance from the Honorable Minister Louis Farrakhan for responding to a not guilty verdict, I knew these words would have great significance and required my full attention. He told me to speak to the world and warn of the wrath of God if Justice is not served. There would be no second chance to deliver the message; therefore, I hoped to be as prepared as possible.

The verdict came so quickly that I was not able to write a single word.

My son, Salih and I rushed into our clothes and headed to court. I made contact with my Brothers and Ministers Tony Muhammad (Los Angeles) and Christopher (San Francisco), and headed to court. On our arrival to court, we found more press than on any other occasion. We rushed to court only to find fewer seats available for the public. The court public relations team did their best to accommodate us, but with the increased security and press corps, some supports were unable to get into court. Even Uncle Bobby, the Grant family spokesman was not permitted into court as he arrived just minutes after the courtroom was closed. The Los Angeles Sheriffs were so concerned with security that it looked like the entire building was being evacuated.

Judge Perry was clearly concerned with public outburst and declared his desire for calm regardless of the verdict. More sheriffs were present than on any other court date. At least 20 officers were present and surrounded the defendant and his family.

As we awaited the final verdict of the jury, we held hands and we prayed.

Judge Perry listened intently as the jury foreman read the verdict. On the charge of second degree murder: not guilty. On the charge of voluntary manslaughter: not guilty. On the charge of involuntary manslaughter: guilty. On the charge of weapons enhancement: guilty.

The following remarks were made by Attorney John Burris, Cephus Johnson, Wanda Johnson and me as we emerged from the court to address the world. We stopped the group from walking straight into the press corps, gathered on another floor to discuss the verdict and made our way to meet the press.

"The next test of course is when and how much time the officer, Mr. Mehserle, is sentenced to jail. Under traditional, regular notions, he should be going to jail for the rest of his life, for the rest of his life, but yet, he very well may get a sentence that does not even require him to go to jail, which would be the ultimate insult and travesty as I could imagine," Attorney John Burris said.

"This really has stuck a dagger in us to a degree to where we know today that we must begin this fight from this point in order to seek justice ... It hurts us as a family to have been going through this the past 19 months to hear that there's a possibility that this man who committed murder may be able to go home and eat dinner after August 6," Mr. Cephus Johnson said after being locked out of the court by sheriffs' for arriving a few moments late for the surprise verdict announcement.

I shared their disappointment that the jury deliberated only for six and a half hours after the family waited for 19 months for justice. This was a travesty of justice itself, but justice cannot be compromised. It was clear that the jury made a compromise. With three charges to consider; second degree murder, voluntary manslaughter, and involuntary manslaughter to discuss, it was unimaginable that a jury of men and women without much legal experience could so quickly resolve the differences in these charges. Judge Perry instructed the jury that before considering any lesser charges, that it must first have unanimous agreement for acquittal on the most serious of charges. The speed of the deliberations made it clear that justice had been compromised.

"Be crystal clear we are not satisfied. Be crystal clear God is not satisfied! It is written in the Bible that God declares that he hears the moaning and the groaning of a people that have endured this kind of suffering for 400 years and that when God hears that kind of suffering know for a surety that if the system of justice will not do justice while it is in the hands of the system of justice to do, that God himself will relieve the suffering of a mother and of a people that have attempted to see that this system would work."

As I spoke, I noticed the media breaking down cameras, avoiding making a record of our complete remarks. However, Oscar's mother, Wanda Johnson, who had not intended to speak felt compelled to speak and this forced the media to continue recording. I pulled her forward to the microphones and she made it plain that she was disappointed with the system of justice in the following remarks:

> "My son was murdered! He was murdered! He was murdered! He was murdered! My son was murdered, and the law has not held the officer accountable the way that he should have been held accountable.

> "Even though this system will fail us and let us down, God will never fail us, nor will he let us down and I will trust in him until I die. ... We wrestle not against flesh and blood but against principalities and powers and spiritual wickedness in high places and we will continue to pray without ceasing because we know that our deliverer, Jesus Christ, the Lord our Savior ... will deliver us."

There was no need to entertain the press with questions. Our position was made clear. Justice had not been achieved and the jury missed the opportunity to make right the wrong of Johannes Mehserle by rendering a just verdict. Justice still stands afar because truth was left on the floor by a jury that compromised justice.

The nineteen month wait for justice left us all dissatisfied. We left the area of the court immediately, not knowing where to go and anxious to get away from court. We went to the comfort of my mother's home in Los Angeles, refreshed and regrouped ourselves, and prepared for the long drive home to the Bay area.

Before we returned home from the verdict, Johannes Mehserle issued an immediate apology letter through his lawyers for the media. This so-called apology to the family was not given to the family. It was to influence Judge Perry to view Mehserle as a man who felt remorse for the killing of Oscar Grant. When we read his letter, it was clear that Mehserle was seeking to affect the judges' sentence and rehabilitate his public image.

Community leaders and the Grant family hosted a press conference outside our weekly Townhall meeting held at True Vine Church in West Oakland the day after the verdict. The press wanted to know if the Grant family had accepted the apology of Mehserle. Cephus Johnson made it clear that Mehserle never apologized to the family; he apologized to the media and made no attempt, ever, to contact the mother and family of Oscar Grant. Therefore, Cephus called Mehserle's letter, "garbage."

To add insult to injury, the media made every effort to get remarks from Cephus and Wanda to denounce the many activists arrested for alleged violence that occurred in Oakland while the family received the bad news of acquittal on the most serious charges against Mehserle. It was unfair of the members of media to hold the Johnson family responsible for the anger that existed in the hearts of many protesters. The protesters had a right to be angry and it was community outrage that brought this case to trial. We all resisted the invitation to make the famed statements of Rodney King-like statement, "Can we all get along?" because the only way to settle the angry hearts of the people is to bring justice. Injustice anywhere is a threat to justice everywhere and if members of the media were concerned about peace, then they should join the family of Oscar Grant and the community in pursuit of justice.

Sentencing Hearing

On November 5th, 2010, we returned for the sentencing of Johannes Mehserle for involuntary manslaughter and weapons charges. A jury of his peers found him guilty of these two crimes. The community, armed with the knowledge that his sentence for these charges could range from probation to 4 years in prison for the involuntary manslaughter charge and an additional 2 to 10 years for the weapons enhancement.

We were left with the unusual position of asking the judge to punish Mehserle with a maximum penalty on the minimal conviction he received. As Wanda said after the verdict, "My son was murdered."

Community activists, along with Cephus, organized a letter writing campaign that produced more than 5,000 letters from persons demanding justice. Many of these letters came from children, who watched video of the news clips that were introduced by Cephus, Jack Bryson, Michael Greer's mother Tracy, Sister Beatrice X and me. Our journey to visit students took us across the country to Howard University, to the South in Watts, California and Bay area cities of San Jose, Berkeley, San Francisco and Oakland.

These meetings and rallies were often hosted by campus Black Student Unions. We found unanimous support for the campaign for justice and thousands of letters began pouring in from students, teachers and administrators to demand justice for the murder of Oscar Grant.

One of the most surprising moments in the trial was Judge Perry's reception and courtroom interpretation of these letters of support. He chose to read parts of some into his final comments before sentencing. Every time he read a letter that referred to the death of Oscar Grant as "murder" he openly winced. He complained again as he acknowledged that one of the letters written came from a school principle declaring that the letter writers got it all wrong. This was not murder, he decried, and if a school principle could get this so wrong, then no wonder there is so much racial tension; he chided the writing effort as misguided. This was not a murder; it was manslaughter.

Sitting in court watching Judge Perry attack the community and family for addressing the killing of Oscar as murder; not involuntary manslaughter seemed to anger Judge Perry. Rather than accept the impact his death had on the community and family of Oscar, Judge Perry argued the validity of our concerns. This was a first slap in the face of the people who only wanted justice.

His next slap in the face of justice was his repeatedly declaring that he was troubled by the jury verdict of guilty on the weapons enhancement charges; the only guilty finding that could have led to mandatory sentencing that could extend Mehserle jail time to a total of 14 years.

He allowed the District Attorney and defense attorneys to argue the question of intent and to guess what the jury intended when it found a guilty verdict for weapons enhancement which the DA interpreted as an intentional act; while the jury also found a guilty verdict for involuntary manslaughter which the defense attorney defined as unintentional.

Certainly, it would be difficult to understand a verdict that says an act is both unintentional (involuntary manslaughter) and intentional (weapons enhancement rules) at the same time. The real question became, how did the judge instruct the jury to handle these issues?

Judge Perry admitted that the jury concluded its fast deliberations just 15 minutes after sending the Judge a question about the weapons charge. Within minutes of the Judge telling them they may include or pursue the weapons charges; the jury returned its verdict: Guilty for involuntary manslaughter and Guilty for weapons use charges.

When we emerged from court on the day of the verdict I called the jury verdict a "compromise". It was clear the jury cut a deal to go home for the weekend and not return and deliberate another day. No jury would have felt good, especially in the city of Los Angeles where Rodney King weighs heavy on the hearts of its citizens, without a conviction that would insure a guilty police officer serve real jail time.

The jury was given 3 charges to deliberate. First the jury had to consider 2nd degree murder. If the jury found unanimous agreement for acquittal; then, and only then, could it consider the next most serious charge of voluntary manslaughter. Second, the jury must deliberate voluntary manslaughter and if the jury unanimously acquits Mehserle of voluntary manslaughter; then, and only then, could the jury consider deliberating the lesser charge of involuntary manslaughter.

The jury must consider the most serious charges first; then, and only then, can the jury move to consider the lesser charge. However, in addition to these 3 potential charges was the weapons enhancement. The jury posed a question. The judge gave an answer. On this day the Judge admitted that he may have given the wrong answer.

To convince the judge of the concerns of the family of the victim and community, the family was invited by the court to offer an impact statement. I was honored to enter a letter along with the family. Several family members were permitted to read their letters or make personal statement in court.

Cephus Johnson would lead off the family impact statements. But Cephus, watching Judge Perry attack the sentiments of the public that he worked so hard to reach with the truth about the murder of Oscar, prefaced his remarks by declaring for the judge that whether he liked it or not, to the Johnson family, this was murder and they would continue to address the crime as a murder. After making his passionate appeal for justice, Cephus (Bobby) concluded with prophetic words of warning, balling his fist, and bravely commanding the attention of the court saying; it would be a shame if Mehserle walk without justice being served because of the error of the court in jury instructions.

Judge Perry admittedly in error on jury instruction, attempted to keep order. He asked Bobby not to raise his voice at him, but that he understood his anger. The judge went further to apologize saying he did the best he could with a difficult case.

Soon, Wanda Johnson would make her appeal. Imagine, appealing to a judge who had earlier demanded your trust in the system, misinformed the jury, and slapped the family in the face from the beginning. Her health began to decline right before our eyes. As tears welled up in her eyes and she pleaded for justice, her voice cracked and her face began to droop, having the appearance of a stroke. The hearts of all in the courtroom with a sense of humanity poured out compassion for a mother whose son had been murdered by an officer who is paid to represent justice. It was apparent the judge was not moved.

After the family impact statements; another attempted apology came from Mehserle. Judge Perry instructed all statements to be directed to the court and not to the family or audience. As a result, we never saw Mehserle's face.

He shot his apology in the back. As he recounted the events of January 1, 2009 he reiterated the common police officer excuse that the shooting was the fault of the victim. If Oscar Grant had complied with instructions, he never would have been in this position. If he had only surrendered his hands, nothing like this would have happened. This accident was because Oscar Grant refused to cooperate. Damn, he really said this in court while "apologizing."

In his final remarks, Judge Perry stated his view of Mehserle. He declared that Mehserle showed tons of remorse. But, he never said what Mehserle was remorseful for. Was his remorse for the pain caused to the

Grant family or because his few weeks in jail caused him to miss his child, born January 2, 2009. Judge Perry could not get into Mehserle's mind. He could only judge his actions and words. How could he have concluded that Mehserle showed tons of remorse?

Johannes Mehserle never made any statement about his role in the murder of Oscar Grant until he was on the witness stand. He never issued an apology until he was convicted; releasing a letter of apology from jail through his attorney. However, the apology was not addressed to the mother and family of Oscar Grant. It was clearly a made for media apology made to influence the judges' view of his remorse.

Judge Perry went on to declare his problem with the jury instructions and the answer he gave to the jury about weapon enhancement charges as they deliberated. He concluded that there was no evidence to conclude that this shooting was other than an accident. He concluded that Oscar Grant was resisting arrest. He ruled that the weapons enhancement charge was not supported by the evidence and dismissed the charges and verdict. He dismissed the greatest part of the potential sentence for Johannes Mehserle.

That would leave the Judge with the option of sentencing Mehserle from simple probation to four years in prison.

Faced with this reality, Wanda could see the handwriting on the wall. She stood up from her seat saying, "he's about to walk. He's gonna let him walk". Wanda got up to leave and so did I. There was no need to hear the judge's final remarks. It was clear that the judge had winked at justice.

Johannes Mehserle was sentenced to two years for the murder of Oscar Grant on the charge of involuntary manslaughter. He was permitted time served and may be home in 7 months with good behavior. Mehserle has not seen a State Penitentiary; his time has been served in protective custody in a County jail.

He is filing an appeal for the involuntary manslaughter charges, stating their fear that a precedent would be set that police can be charged and convicted for an "accidental" shooting.

Remember, it's been 400 years that Blacks have suffered from United States, British, and other European gangsters, banksters and their colonial police forces which supported and participated in multiple mob attacks against a people who have done them no wrong. Approximately 400 times per year, police are involved in fatal shootings. A little over 40% of those killed are Black men. No police officer in the history of this country has ever been convicted of murder. Who would convict a slave-master for killing his own slave? That would set a dangerous precedent.

1. Why were city officials so concerned with outsiders who came to Oakland to protest the murder of Oscar Grant?
2. How was the Reverend Dr. Martin Luther King, Jr. treated when he came to Birmingham, Alabama to demand justice by church leaders? (Study his famous "Letter from a Birmingham Jail")
3. Why didn't the family respond positively to the Mehserle apology letter?
4. How did Judge Perry respond to the letters of the community demanding justice? Why did so many persons write their feeling about this case to Judge Perry?

Keith Muhammad, Wanda Johnson, Kenny Johnson, and Cephus Johnson address Los Angeles press.
Photo: Jamo Muhammad

Chapter 12
Justice

What is Justice?

The Honorable Elijah Muhammad declared in his 1959 message at Uline Arena, "Justice is a common thing. Yet it is elusive." This journey we travel finds us in constant pursuit of an elusive justice. We have taken our case to many forums and courts. Our demands have been made and heard in the California State Government, before members of Congress, before the BART Board of Directors, before members and participants of the Congressional Black Caucus, before the Obama Administration and the Department of Justice.

Though we have travelled long distances attempting to secure it, justice still appears elusive. The family of Oscar Grant is still in court seeking Justice. While many may wonder what this will cost BART, in reality, the family is not satisfied with simple monetary settlements. Surely they did not see their son's life in monetary terms. What is the value of human life? What price should be paid for unjustifiable taking of human life?

In America, whose law enforcement agencies have a history rooted in slave catching, what is the value of the life of a Black man? Is his life worthy of equal protection under the law? Should a Black man, killed by the same authority that was born to catch him attempting to be free, be equally protected from the misconduct of those in authority?

Will America ever answer for declaring our people lawful captives? Will America ever answer for the countless millions who lost their lives in the Middle Passage? Will America ever answer for the countless millions tortured into submission, and forced out of their names, language, religion, culture, history and God? Will America answer for declaring the Black man to be worth only 3/5 of a human being? Will America answer for the thousands of lynching victims whose lives were never protected by law? We have waited hundreds of years and justice has been elusive.

The Bible teaches, wait on the Lord. Yet, we should know that this does not imply that we wait on the Lord to do all things while we do nothing.

James 5:6-8 (King James Version)

⁶Ye have condemned and killed the just; and he doth not resist you.

⁷Be patient therefore, brethren, unto the coming of the Lord. Behold, the husbandman waiteth for the precious fruit of the earth, and hath long patience for it, until he receive the early and latter rain.

⁸Be ye also patient; stablish your hearts: for the coming of the Lord draweth nigh.

The Bibles' many lessons on patience are needed to protect our spirit as we pursue justice. Court prosecutions take time. Legislative changes take time. Policy, procedure, and training changes take time. Each of these practical steps requires work. Faith without work is dead. The Holy Qur'an adds an additional view of the virtue called patience.

Sabr is an Arabic word meaning "patience." Yet this patience does not mean that we lay back and wait on a mystery God to bring us justice. The Arabic word "sabr" implies many shades of meaning, which is impossible to comprehend in one English word. According to the Yusef Ali translation of the Holy Quran, the meaning of patience includes: 1) the sense of being thorough, not hasty; 2) perseverance, constancy, steadfastness, firmness of purpose; 3) systematic as opposed to spasmodic or chance action; and 4) a cheerful attitude of resignation and understanding in sorrow, defeat, or suffering, as opposed to murmuring or rebellion, but saved from mere passivity or listlessness, by the element of constancy or steadfastness (Footnote 62).

As we have pursued justice, we have organized members of the community including elected officials, activists and family members to do all that we can. Our patience in waiting on the Lord does not mean wait until the Afterlife to see the benefits of our struggle. Sabr is patience that implies work.

In his wise counsel to us, the Honorable Minister Louis Farrakhan has repeatedly instructed us to do all that we can. We are in pursuit of justice, and therefore every avenue for justice is being addressed. This journey has taken us to government at every level possible, to give the government a chance to get it right. We did this because God never punishes the wicked without first giving those whose actions are offensive to Him the opportunity to repent and atone.

Will America repent?

Repentance is a divine principle found in many faith traditions. It permits the sinner to effectively seek the forgiveness of God and the persons offended by our sin. The repentant person is not too proud to admit, to confess, to acknowledge his sin. The repentant person feels sorrow for their sin, sorrow for offending God, and sorrow for his affect on others. The repentant believer is willing to sacrifice all they have to God to regain His favor. God never asks His worshippers to submit partially; He wants entire submission from us. Consider the following passages from the Bible:

Joel 2:11-13 (New King James Version)

11 The LORD gives voice before His army,
For His camp is very great;
For strong *is the One* who executes His word.
For the day of the LORD *is* great and very terrible;
Who can endure it?

A Call to Repentance

12 " Now, therefore," says the LORD,

" Turn to Me with all your heart,
With fasting, with weeping, and with mourning."
13 So rend your heart, and not your garments;
Return to the LORD your God,
For He *is* gracious and merciful,
Slow to anger, and of great kindness;
And He relents from doing harm.

Luke 5:31-33 (New King James Version)

31 Jesus answered and said to them, "Those who are well have no need of a physician, but those who are sick. 32 I have not come to call *the* righteous, but sinners, to repentance."

Jeremiah 8:5-7 (New King James Version)

5 Why has this people slidden back,
Jerusalem, in a perpetual backsliding?

They hold fast to deceit,
They refuse to return.
 ⁶ I listened and heard,
But they do not speak aright.
No man repented of his wickedness,
Saying, 'What have I done?'
Everyone turned to his own course,
As the horse rushes into the battle.
 ⁷ " Even the stork in the heavens
Knows her appointed times;
And the turtledove, the swift, and the swallow
Observe the time of their coming.
But My people do not know the judgment of the LORD.

During his trial, Johannes Mehserle was silent on how badly he felt about the shooting of Oscar Grant and the impact it has had on the Johnson family. As remorseful as he claimed to be, he spent much more time crying over his temporary separation away from his child caused by the trial. It is understandable that as a father, he wanted more quality time with his child, however, justice remains afar. Wanda Johnson, for the rest of her life, will never have another day to sit with Oscar, to ride in a car with Oscar, to dine with Oscar or just to laugh and cry with Oscar.

As history shows, Judge Robert Perry was evidently impressed. In his final sentencing of Mehserle, Judge Perry attempted to address the family and community's feelings that Mehserle was unapologetic. Perry declared that Mehserle had shown "tons of remorse."

From the time of Oscar's death and throughout the trial, Mehserle had not shared an ounce of his remorse with the Grant family. His legal strategy appeared to be to fight the views of the Grant family. From the beginning of the trial through its conclusion, Mehserle blamed Oscar for the shooting by suggesting that if Oscar had complied with his orders, that he would have never "accidently" pulled the wrong weapon. In other words, it's not my fault that I shot him on "accident," but instead he brought this on himself. Where is the repentance? What happened to the apology? It was lost in the effort to be relieved of punishment for his actions. An apology that is not sincerely made is an apology that cannot produce sincere atonement and forgiveness.

Cephus Johnson was honest, sincere and angry. He challenged Judge Perry for making errors that would permit Johannes Mehserle to have his sentence reduced to a minimum, after Oscar Grant had paid the ultimate price for the deed of Johannes Mehserle.

Judge Perry clearly desired that Mehserle and his ruling be received well, but he knew that would not be the case. He concluded the case by dismissing the jury's conviction of weapons charges, thereby relieving Mehserle of the possibility of a mandatory prison term of 10 years. Judge Perry further supported police contentions that Oscar Grant resisted arrest, and that if he had not resisted arrest, then none of this may have ever happened. It appeared as though Mehserle hired Judge Perry to emphasize his argument beyond the ability of his own attorney, Michael Rains. It was as if Judge Perry, Mehserle and Rains were brothers, defending one another without regard to right or wrong, justice or injustice.

In the Hoy Qur'an, Believers are guided to stand on truth, even if the truth is against our own selves, our family and our friends. Our faith demands that we stand on principles of truth. This may be why Jesus declared his mother and his brother were in the Temple with him. For Jesus, those who were striving with him to stand on principles of truth were more important than blood relations. Accordingly, Jesus is said to be the son of David according to the flesh, and yet he is declared the Son of God according to the Spirit of Holiness. His Spirit is more significant than his earthly relationships.

Holy Qur'an 4:135

> *O you who believe, be maintainers of justice, bearers of witness for Allah, even though it be against your own selves or (your) parents or near relatives — whether he be rich or poor, Allah has a better right over them both. So follow not (your) low desires, lest you deviate. And if you distort or turn away from (truth), surely Allah is ever Aware of what you do.*

Justice is Coming

The Honorable Elijah Muhammad writes,

"Men have sought its meaning and substance since time began. Plato shrugged that justice was nothing more than the wish of the strongest members of society. Jesus equated justice with brotherhood. Shakespeare saw it as a matter of mercy. I am here to tell you that justice is the eventual working out of the will of God as indicated in the fundamental principles of truth. Justice is the antithesis of wrong, the weapon God will use to bring judgment upon the world, the purpose and consummation of His coming."

God comes to bring justice. This is profound. If He comes to bring justice, then those who suffer injustice are the objects of His intervention. He intervenes into the lives of a people who have been deprived of justice. The Honorable Elijah Muhammad went further to state that, "had justice prevailed, there would be no need for a day of judgment to come today, not to the unjust judges of the world, but to the just judge to give the Black man of America justice."

Judge Robert Perry presided over the case of the State of California vs. Johannes Mehserle. I am clear that while he presides over the court ruled by modern government, he does not preside over the court of God. This is evident through his refusal to accept or acknowledge the historical pain of the Grant family and community, swift dismissal of complaints for the suffering of the people, declaration that he would wait out the protesters, argument against the jury verdict, reversal of his own jury instructions, and dismissal of the jury verdict which would have insured greater jail time for the first police officer in the history of California convicted for killing while on duty. All of this makes clear to me that we must rely on a power greater than the court of California for our solution.

The Honorable Elijah Muhammad declared in his seminal book, "Message to the Blackman," in chapter 103 entitled "Our Day is Near at Hand":

> "Every day of our lives we are at your mercy. An army of policemen throughout the country with clubs in their hands set out to beat the "nigger" and to shoot the "nigger" if they feel like it."

> "Nothing is hindering him. He is not going to go to prison for doing it. All he has to do is to tell the judge that he shot that old "nigger" and the judge will wink his eye at him and say, "Wish I had a chance to shoot him myself. This is the kind of people we are living with. With murderers, not friends, but murderers."

Throughout this trial, I found myself for signs of winks exchanged between the judge and the defendant. Mehserle faced the judge throughout the trial. When Mehserle gave his remorse statement, the Judge instructed him not to face the family, but to direct all his comments to the judge. I wondered whether they exchanged winks during that testimony. Judge Perry's conclusion strongly suggests they did. The Honorable Elijah Muhammad's words fit this trial perfectly. The system of justice apparently had no intentions of healing the hearts of a family and suffering Black community that has waited 400 years for the system to treat with fairness and equity.

I, along with thousands of others, addressed a letter to Judge Perry to appeal to his heart and sense of justice for the murder of Oscar Grant. The family honored me by submitting my letter along with the other letters by family members. The Honorable Minister Louis Farrakhan guided me in the process, read my letter, and advised me not to expect too much from Judge Perry. He said to me that to get this judge to do the right thing with letters would be like getting water from a rock. In other words, Judge Perry represents a system of hardened hearts. Pray for the best, but do not be surprised by the worst. Judge Perry's conclusion reflected the latter. The family and all those who sacrificed for this struggle for justice received the worst from this system, and justice remains afar.

We have introduced this case to the U.S. Department of Justice and requested their review. God willing, the Department will bring charges against Johannes Mehserle and his accomplices for violation of the civil rights of Oscar Grant III and his friends. If, however, the Department fails to perform its duty of insuring equal protection under the laws of America, then we know that God sees, God knows, and God is the ultimate Judge of humanity. Regardless of the actions of government, Almighty God will rule with truth and justice. The Journey to Justice for Oscar Grant has grown beyond merely a civil rights case. The case of Oscar Grant represents a matter of divine human rights, and the truth is now being weighed in Court presided over by the real Judge, God Himself.

May ALLAH (God) bless us all in the Journey for Justice.

1. What is justice?
2. Why did the Grant family reject the apology letter?
3. Why is the coming of God to bring justice considered profound?
4. How did the Honorable Elijah Muhammad view the relationship between police brutality and courtroom judgments?
5. Why did the family and community appeal to the U.S. Department of Justice to investigate the murder of Oscar Grant?

Attorney John Burris, Cephus Johnson, and Jack Bryson on sentencing for Johannes Mehserle.

Lessons Learned Fighting for Justice in the Murder of Oscar Grant

Timeline

January 1, 2009

Oscar Grant is slain by BART Officer Johannes Mehserle while traveling home from a News Years celebration in San Francisco.

January 6, 2009

Concerned clergy leaders, politicians and activists meet at Olivet Institutional Missionary Baptist Church to discuss the murder of Oscar Grant and plan to challenge District Attorney Tom Orloff to bring charges against Johannes Mehserle for murder.

January 7, 2009

On the morning of the funeral for Oscar Grant, community activists and elected officials hold a press conference on the steps of the Alameda County Courthouse and demand a meeting with the District Attorney.

Protesters gather at Fruitvale BART to demand justice for Oscar Grant. A splinter group broke away and marched toward downtown Oakland, was confronted by police lines and the rebellion begins, concluding with Mayor Dellums attempt to calm a crowd that would eventually destroy property and close dozens of businesses.

January 8, 2009

Mayor Dellums hosts a press conference declaring the city's intention to instruct OPD to investigate. Joining Mayor Dellums was District Attorney Tom Orloff, Police Commanders and members of the community.

January 13, 2009

Johannes Mehserle arrested in Nevada.

January 14, 2009

Protesters march in Oakland from City Hall to the Alameda County Courthouse. Included in the protest are Mayor Dellums, Councilperson Brooks, Rapper Too Short, and dozens others. The evening erupts in violence.

January 30, 2009

A judge said today that he set a high bail of $3 million for former Bay Area Rapid Transit police Officer Johannes Mehserle because he thinks Mehserle gave an "inconsistent story" about why he shot and killed Oscar Grant III.

February 17, 2009

Historic Oakland Town hall meeting presents the Honorable Minister Louis Farrakhan

February 19, 2009

Caravan for Justice I takes hundreds of activists from Northern California to demand justice for Oscar Grant and justice for the voiceless oppressed masses of California

March 18, 2009

Lovelle Mixon, after a traffic stop in Oakland, shoots and kills four members of the Oakland Police Department.

Judge Don C. Clay postponed a March 21 preliminary hearing Monday for Johannes Mehserle after a defense attorney expressed concern about the case going to court in the aftermath of the killings of four Oakland police officers over the weekend. Mehserle's attorney, Michael Rains, told Judge he feared that tensions over the slayings of the Oakland officers might be inflamed by what he says will be an aggressive defense of Mehserle.

April 8, 2009

Caravan for Justice II takes over 1000 activists from Northern California to demand justice for Oscar Grant and justice for the voiceless oppressed masses of California

May 28, 2009

Caravan for Justice III takes over 2000 activists from Northern and Southern California. The delegation, hundreds of whom entered the legislature, were acknowledged in the public record by Assemblyman Sandre' Swanson

June 4, 2009

After a week of hearings, Judge Don C. Clay orders Johannes Mehserle to stand trial for murder; he became the first police officer in California history to stand trial for an on-duty killing

September 11, 2009

Johannes Mehserle files for motion to change the venue of his trial out of Alameda County

October 16, 2009

Judge Morris Jacobson grants the Change of Venue motion filed by Johannes Mehserle

June 2, 2010

Opening Arguments in Los Angeles Trial for Johannes Mehserle

June 16, 2010

Assembly Bill 1586 (Swanson) is sign into law by California Governor Swartzenegger, permitting BART to implement a Citizen Review Board to oversee police abuse allegations.

July 8, 2010

The Verdict: Guilty of Involuntary Manslaughter with a Weapons Enhancement, acquittal for Second degree murder and voluntary manslaughter. Mehserle releases an apology letter through the press.

November 5, 2010

Johannes Mehserle is sentenced to two years minus time served. Judge Robert Perry dismissed charges for weapons enhancement, making it possible for Mehserle to return home early summer 2011.

January 2011

The U.S. Department of Justice has picked up files for the Mehserle case to consider if the rights of Oscar Grant were violated.

Cephus Johnson meets Congressman John Conyers at the Congressional Black Caucus weekend to encourage him to watch the case closely as chairman of the House Judiciary Committee.
Photo: Karrima Muhammad